The Aryballos as an Example

The Corinthian Aryballos as a mirror of the artistic
connections between East and West in
the 8th to the 6th centuries BC – an artistic analysis

Amnon Dvir

BAR International Series 2315
2011

Published in 2019 by
BAR Publishing, Oxford

BAR International Series 2315

The Aryballos as an Example

© Amnon Dvir and the Publisher 2011

COVER IMAGE *Proto-Corinthian Aryballos from Thebes. Work by Painter 'Macmillan', mid 7th century BC (According to VA IZOA Greek Art, Sheldon Nodelman)*

ISBN 9781407308982 paperback
ISBN 9781407338781 e-book

DOI https://doi.org/10.30861/9781407308982

A catalogue record for this book is available from the British Library

This book is available at www.barpublishing.com

BAR Publishing is the trading name of British Archaeological Reports (Oxford) Ltd.
British Archaeological Reports was first incorporated in 1974 to publish the BAR
Series, International and British. In 1992 Hadrian Books Ltd became part of the BAR
group. This volume was originally published by Archaeopress in conjunction with
British Archaeological Reports (Oxford) Ltd / Hadrian Books Ltd, the Series principal
publisher, in 2011. This present volume is published by BAR Publishing, 2019.

BAR

PUBLISHING

BAR titles are available from:

BAR Publishing
122 Banbury Rd, Oxford, OX2 7BP, UK
EMAIL   info@barpublishing.com
PHONE   +44 (0)1865 310431
FAX   +44 (0)1865 316916
www.barpublishing.com

PROLOGUE

Despite having been educated on the traditions of the classic world for many years, I have always been inclined, as will my veteran tutors gladly testify, to delve into pre-classic roots. The search for significant connections from the early eastern and Aegean past, to the archaic and classic Greece, has always guided me in my research of the artistic component and its characteristic analysis. I hope that my study of the Corinthian Aryballos will serve as testimony to the weightiness of primordial cultural cargoes and their subsequent expressive significance, as well as satisfying the cumulated expectations of my research predilection.

I take this occasion to hereby express my thanks and appreciation to Prof. Israel Roll and Prof. Moshe Fisher for their assistance throughout the period of my work.

I also commend the university libraries at the Tel Aviv and Haifa Universities that provided the required research literature and documents, and my thanks to Simcha Zaharur for all her assistance. Then of course are the numerous services provided by the library at the Eretz Israel Museum in Tel Aviv and especially the assistance provided by Etiana Felix and Zvika Shaham.

This work is dedicated to my beloved father Simcha Dvir
 and Prof' Israel Roll - R.I.P,
To my beloved Mother, Lonya Dvir, Yehudit, Ruth and my son Noam - may live long life
Special thanks to Prof' A. Segal for his warm support.

Amnon Dvir
December 2010

LIST OF ABBREVIATIONS

AASOR	*Annual of the American Schools of Oriental Research*
AJA	*American Journal of Archaeology*
ANET	*Ancient Near Eastern Texts Relating to the Old Testament (J.B. Pritchard, Ed.)*
BA	*The Biblical Archaeologist*
Barnett, Catalogue	*R. D. Barnett, A Catalogue of the Nimrud Ivories in the British Museum* (London 1975)
BASOR	*Bulletin of American Schools of Oriental Research*
BCH	*Bulletin de Correspondance Hellenique*
BICS	*Bulletin of the Institute of Classical Studies (London)*
BMB	*Bulletin du Musée de Beyrouth (1937-)*
BMQ	*Museum Quarterly,* London *British* (from 1926)
BSA	*Annual of the British School at Athens*
CCO	*The Cretan Collection in Oxford. J. Boardman (1961)*
CIS	*Corpus Inscriptionum Semiticarum (Paris 1881-)*
CVA	*Corpus Vasorum Antiquorum*
IEJ	*Israel Exploration Journal*
JHS	*Journal of Hellenic Studies*
JNES	*Journal of Near Eastern Studies*
KAI	*Kanaanäische und aramäische Inschriften,* (H. Donner & W. Röllig Eds.), Vols. I-III, Wiesbaden 1966-1969.
Moscati, Catalogue	Ed. S. Moscati, *The Phoenicians* Venezia 1988)
RA	*Revue Archéologique*
RB	*Revue Biblique*
RDAC	*Report of the Department of Antiquities, Cyprus*
RSF	*Rivista di Studi Fenici*
SIMA	*Studies in Mediterranean Archaeology*
SPV	*Studia Phoenicia, Vol. V (Phoenicia and the East Mediterranean in the 1st Millennium B.C)* Ed. E. Lipinski, 1987

INTRODUCTION

The Corinthian Aryballos, a perfume vessel, is the subject of this book. I shall examine the place of the Corinthian Aryballos within the cultural system of ties between East and West. Through an exhaustive artistic analysis of the vessel and all its characteristics, I shall attempt to prove that the Aryballos can serve as a measure of the period between the 8th and 6th centuries BC. Corinth during the said period was a dominant center of ceramics production, more so than any other important center, such as Crete or Cyprus.[1] Dunbabin (1962:11) regards Corinth as a primary source of the Aryballoi, i.e., the ultimate origin.

According to Dunbabin trade between Greece and the Orient during the 8th century BC was direct and not necessarily through Crete or Cyprus. According to the results of researching findings from Corinth, Attica and Crete, Corinth was found to be the leading manufacturer of the vessel and the center of cultural development characterized by an interesting combination of increasingly flourishing trade and art. Both Athens and Crete copied the Corinthian model.

Up until the colonial expansion of Corinth and the massive use of perfumes from the orient, there was very little use of the Aryballoi. It derived from Corinth's increasing array of connections with the orient and the increased use of perfumes from the East, which opened and enriched the trade routes and naturally the demand for that specific vessel, in turn increasing its distribution.[2] It is also important to fundamentally examine the development of this special vessel in terms of shape and especially the integration of certain decorations and paintings on this vessel alongside an examination of artistic parallels and comparison thereto within various contexts. I also intend to expand the peripheral circumference of this research through an interpretative discussion of possible friction between the factors and its implication, in a chapter titled: Corinth and the Phoenician Connection.

Several decades prior to the comprehensive studies conducted by Johansen (1923) and Payne (1931, 1933), Willisch (1982; see also Amyx 1988:355) studied the Corinthian ceramic matter and attempted for the first time to summarize his research systematically. Initial

precedents to the study of Aryballoi in their primary form, prior to the ovoid shape, i.e. the globular Aryballoi and those typical of the transition period (see details of vessel shapes and chronological tables see p. 48) was first diagnosed by Orsi in 1893 (see Neeft 1987:17).

Johansen preceded his time with an important study of Sikyonion vessels, despite having been mistaken in the location, assuming that Sikyon served as the origin of Proto-Corinthian vessels. Johansen differentiated an additional type of Aryballos, the conical or the "piriform" type (Johansen 1923:16), in researching the technique and pattern of decoration of the Aryballoi with the "black-figure" decoration. Johansen showed that the different types of decorations testify to stages in development of the vessel with the same shape. He determined the sub-Geometric terminology because the unique style bore new motifs, different to those that appear during the Geometric period and therefore their chronological position is at the end of the period. Despite this, he did not in fact separate the Aryballoi with the sub-Geometric decoration from those with the figures decorations because the vessels themselves were of similar shape (Johansen 1923:22ff, 163, 178-185).

According to this study by Johansen and through Schweitzer, an additional researcher of the period (Schweitzer, 1918),[3] the chronological table, on which future researches were based, was determined. Schweizer positioned the beginning of the globular Aryballos development at 750 BC.

The comprehensive and important study by Humphrey Payne (1931) determined the Corinthian origin of the Aryballos, i.e. the original workshop.[4] In Payne's general study of the Corinthian ceramic pottery and later of the Proto-Corinthian ceramic material (Payne 1933) he differentiated between groups of painters and solitary painter and even dealt with diagnosing set styles and secondary divisions, however (mainly due to lack of documentation) he did not enrich the study with names of the painters. Payne placed the end of the Proto-Corinthian Aryballos period at around 625 BC based on the finding from Selinus (Payne 1931:22ff, 1933:20).

Payne even emphasized the sub-Geometric decorative style characteristic: the animal (silhouette) style, which is not associated with the Linear Style. Hopper (1949) also claims that the silhouette style belongs to this period and is different from the decorations emphasized with engraving. This style also appears later and its components do not essentially characterize the Geometric period.

---

[1] Where the Aryballos appeared at an earlier stage, during the 9th-8th centuries BC, probably through increased interaction with the east. Some researchers negate the origin of the vessel's local production, claiming it was imported from the Aegean region. Dunbabin 1962:11 n. 2.

[2] On the increased use of perfumes from the east and the flourishing of the trade routes along which they reached pre-classical Greece, see De Romanis 1996: 33-70; for the flourishing trade routes, see Sherratt 1993:361-378 – the beginning of activity along the route Levante-Cyprus-Euboeia and Crete during the 10-9th centuries BC and the important parallel "trans-isthmian" route (that included Chalcis- Eretria-Athens-Corinth-Argos) during the 8-7th centuries BC. These routes and their western counterparts (see Aubet 1993) during the said period, there was highly significant Phoenician naval activity. See also the learned remarks by Whitley (2001:103-133) on this subject.

[3] Neeft 1987:17, n. 10, Johansen 1923:179-185, Schweitzer 1918:34, relying in addition on the dates of ancient sources written about the Greek settlements in Sicily and Southern Italy during the 7th-8th centuries BC.

[4] In researching the origins, he looked for influences from Crete. Payne 1931:35-42 and see Neeft 1987:17, n.12.

Weinberg (1943, 1949)[5] determined the start of the Proto-Corinthian style framework at a relatively later date, 725 BC, whereas Dunbabin (1962, and see later) determined an almost identical chronological framework to that of Payne based on Weinberg.

Francois Villard (1948) in his referral to the beginning of the style phases during the Orientalizing period in Corinth, set the beginning of the process at 710 BC in order to compare and adapt the parallel development in Attica. He discerned the last ovoid phase of the Proto-Corinthian Aryballos because the vessel in this shape was found together with Corinthian vessels from the Early Corinthian period (see Early Corinthian in chronological tables).[6]

The classification and presentation of consolidated groups of Aryballoi according to the currently available format began with the important work by Lo Porto (1959/60), which deals with a research of grave contents from Taranto.[7] Dunbabin's important study and his conclusions concerning the ceramic material at the Hera Limenaia temple in Perachora (Dunbabin 1962) enriched the study especially concerning the earlier phase of the Proto-Corinthian ceramic material and particularly that of the Aryballoi.

Dunbabin attributes the animal silhouettes style to second and third quarters of the 7th century BC (Dunbabin 1962 II:8), which appeared alongside the incised style, and in any event, at a period later to the Geometric period. Like Coldstream (1968:104), he uses the term Linear style to differentiate and separate it from another style. Both are of the opinion that the technique and tradition of the Geometric period continue and spill over into a later period, a subject that is discussed below in the chapter dealing with the artistic analysis.

Coldstream (1968:93, 95, 97,101 and later 1977) on the basis of his research on Geometric Greek ceramic determines the framework of the Proto-Corinthian period at 720-630 BC.

This is the time to mention the studies by Schefold (1966, 1967) that deal with the subject of the myth in analyzing the artistic components of Greek art and its implications on the ceramic material and in connections with various motifs in the art centers of countries neighboring Greece. Also, I would mention Benson (1971:83-85) that determined chronological boundaries in his research of the active and creative field in the works of the painter Oberdan, who worked during the period of parallel styles, the black-figure and the silhouettes styles.

Later, Neeft (1987) in his analytical and in-depth research of early sub-Geometric Aryballoi excelled in differentiating between the black-figure style and that characteristic of the sub-Geometric period. In his opinion the terminology that defines the animal silhouettes style or the Linear style was designed to enable additional secondary decorative styles and mainly in order to emphasize the existence of an additional developmental element in the form of animal decoration. Based on past studies Neeft surveys the entire vessels and separates between streams, groups and types of vessels through a organized emphasis of their formative and decorative expression.

Some time afterwards the great work by Amyx (1988) was published, a comprehensive and exhaustive survey of the subject of Corinthian vase paintings during the Archaic period. Within the storehouse of information and the corpus framework, Amyx focuses on general subjects (technique, decorative styles, distribution and additional origins, characteristic decorative subjects, etc.), associated with the research, and delays at times over the Aryballoi, particularly as primary and more earlier vessels expressing the interesting development process of the Corinthian ceramics.

Two additional works by Neeft and Amyx (Neeft 1991, Amyx 1996 together with Patricia Lawrence)[8] complete the previous studies at a later stage. The works by these two latter researchers are important for understanding the background and basis for my research, discussed in this book, the one for systematic and specific research of a defined period and the second for comprehensive and large research, although they do not examine the orientalizing process as a leading subject in their studies and do not mention or linger over the conceptual significances of the oriental connection in their works.

Several additional studies supplement interesting subjects associated with the work of the craftsmen in the Corinthian potteries, such as the study by Karen Manchester (1991) on the Proto-Corinthian black polychrome technique.

Other studies that deal with artistic subjects associated with the beginning of the process of presenting figures from Greek mythology at its early stage – in art in general and in ceramics in particular (Jenkins 2002, Ahlberg-Cornell 1992) complete the picture and enrich the background for our period. I shall add the article by Williams (2002) concerning the Alabstron vessel, as an interesting parallel at a later stage and in continuation with the framework to be presented in this book.

During the course of the work, and particularly in the chapter 'Corinth and the Phoenician Connection', the use of the comprehensive and educated study by several

---

[5] In his comprehensive work on the geometric ceramics and of the Orientalizing period in Corinth, however in an earlier study he already determined his diagnosis. See Weinberg 1941:35.

[6] And placed it at 615 BC. See Villard 1948:27,33 and Neeft 1987:18.

[7] Additional studies accumulated following excavations at various sites in Rhodes such as Jalysos, as well as Kameiros and Selinus at Villar 1948, Hopper 1949 and Neeft 1987:18, n.17.

[8] Neeft 1987 in referring to the work by Amyx 1988, and in these latest studies: Amyx & Lawrence 1996 – as an addition to "The Chimaera Group at Corinth": Lawrence 1996, 7, *Corinth VII, ii (1975)* on the activities of the Corinthian workshop and its relationship with Athens.

researchers such as Aubet (1996) Shanks (1999),[9] as well as Whitley (2001) should be added, who used the Aryballos as an element of primary implication for a wider survey, in the chapter dealing with the extent of oriental "influence" in Greece within framework of the "Orientalizing phenomenon" as defined by him.[10] Other specific studies as well, such as those by Morris (1998), Niemeyer (2003) and Stampolidis (2003) deal among others in the reciprocity between Mediterranean basin cultures during the said period.

For example, Burkert's conclusion concerning Olympia (Burkert 1992:4) (Burkert is referring to a fact that indicates previous research flaws concerning Olympia) can be taken as a guiding quotation: "The fact that Olympia is the most significant location for finds of eastern bronzes, richer in this respect than all the Middle Eastern sites, is seldom mentioned". If we connect his conclusion to the main discussion of this book, we will add significant weight to the study focus in Corinth and particularly to the oriental connection and its expression in the chosen vessel and its substantial characteristics. It is also important to put other facts in Corinth and in Gortyn, Crete, up for discussion, on which Burkert (1992:22) adds and lingers, for example with the appearance of a large number of clay figures and statuettes in the mold technique that arrived from Mesopotamia and Syria. A discussion of the latter connects and teaches us about the very productive production centers of sets of vessels and schools from the orient or originating from the orient and the importance of their weight concerning other subjects such as that learned and studied in this paper.[11]

In light of the studies presented above and according to situation of researches dealing with Greek ceramics, it can be assumed that the Aryballos serves as an essential component for understanding the system of connection with the orient that determined its uniqueness. In my opinion it even symbolizes the preferences and demands of the local population, the creative artists and craftsmen, in their attitude towards vessels from the orient and their characteristics, i.e. their role and accompanying decorations.

Through the survey of the existing vessels and the selection of desired patterns, the principle objective of this work is examined, which is, to observe - through a more comprehensive and in-depth artistic analysis of the

vessel and all accompanying components – the characteristics of the Orientalizing process that occurred. Being that I have based this work on the typology of previous studies, this paper will not include any sorting, classification and distribution system of these vessels. These have been expressed and discussed in the works and studies that have been mentioned.

---

[9] The researcher uses, among others, the Aryballos as a representative vessel to establish his views. His work was published three years after outlining my research and writing my paper. The same applies for Whitley, see below.

[10] The survey in Chapter 6: "The Aegean, the Levant and the West: the Orientalizing Phenomenon", states for example the subject of using the engraving technique practiced in oriental metal works such as the Phoenician plates and other subjects my work deals in.

[11] Mention can also be made of the connection to the sources indicated by the Burkert (1992:23) concerning foreign craftsmen required in Greece such as the "public workers", demiourgoi, required in Corinth during the Tyrants period (Herodotes II, 167, 2, or the technitai – for the parallel term in Athens at Diodoros II, 43,3) and see the chapter "Corinth and the Phoenician Connection"

A. THE CORINTHIAN ARYBALLOS – CHARACTERISTICS: THE FORM, THE DECORATION AND DETERMINING THE CHRONOLOGICAL SCHEME

Unlike his Proto-Attic art contemporaries of the late Geometric period, the Proto-Corinthian artist absorbed and assimilated imported Oriental motifs, transferring them to various types of ceramic vessels: more closed, such as the Lekythoi, and smaller, such as the Pyxides and the **Arballoi**, in which he invested his greatest skills and craftsmanship, as shall be shown in the following [12].

A.1 THE PROTO-CORINTHIAN PERIOD

Determining chronology according to an analysis of the Corinthian ceramic in the late Geometric period and during the early Archaic period or the Proto-Corinthian period,[13] is done by classification of the Proto-Corinthian material, focused on the Aryballos, which can serve as the basis for organized and systematic research more so than any other vessel (see Amyx 1988 Vol. III:436, Neeft 1987:17[14]).

The Aryballoi, dating mainly from the early Archaic period, were preserved in excellent condition because of their shape and size and can therefore also be analyzed and diagnosed with relative effectiveness and precision.
It should be noted that throughout the Archaic period Attic vessels express defined style formats as well as a more orderly development, allowing for a rich and detailed analysis.[15] By comparison, Corinthian potters present less gradual development, characterized as follows: the sudden breakthrough and appearance of new, no less interesting, styles. In any event, it is actually the Proto-Corinthian Aryballos that shows consistent elements that enable the construction of a proper developmental framework.

In general, as said, Corinthian vessels, to differ from Attic ones, are much smaller. Corinthian ceramics places greater emphasis on vessels designed for cosmetic uses, oil and perfume containers, such as the Aryballoi and the Alabastra, as well as the Pyxides for storing jewelry and other small decorative ornaments. The plates, bowls and cups as well as the larger vessels such as the Kraters, the Oinochoai, the Kylikes and the Kotylai, associated with wine and drinking, were also common and were also "borrowed" by the Attic potters, notably at the beginning of the 6th century BC. During this century, in its second and third quarters, the trend turned about and the Attic style became dominant, influencing other centers.[16]

As said, the size of these vessels and the craftsman's technique in forming the decorative scheme, provided clear development differentiation and they can therefore de defined and divided relatively conveniently with the proper terminology.

During this period (the end of the Geometric period and the beginning of the early Archaic period, Proto-Corinthian) the Aryballoi can be differentiated by form (see p. 48): the globular (or pansu according to Johansen 1923, and see following) Aryballos, the conical or transitu Aryballos, the ovoid or egg shaped, and the pointed or piriform. Differentiation for chronological determination was based more on the size and shape of the vessels and less on their decorations. Most of the Proto-Corinthian Aryballoi are simply decorated, however there is an internal division based on development of the Aryballos quality with the figurative decoration, which will be elaborated on in the following pages.

An analysis of these vessels from the transitional period between the Geometric and Archaic period, or as it is referred to by researchers – the Proto-Corinthian sub-Geometric Aryballoi, terminology provided by Johansen (Johansen 1923: 72-73) or later, by Neeft in his in-depth, comprehensive and systematic study of the subject (Neeft 1987) was designed to differentiate the ceramics of the said period, to divide and rank it by developmental stages. In other words: the style and technique retain the geometric tradition but belong to a later period and new decorative motifs appear that enrich the vessels ornamentally according to size and shape.[17] Payne (1931:23) attributes the term sub-Geometric to the silhouette style, mainly of animal decorations, to differentiate it from the linear term.[18]

The transition from the Geometric to the Archaic period is also characterized by a graduated change in decorative style.

The Orientalizing period decorative style tempered the earlier harsh local geometric line.[19] During the Geometric period there are two distinct types of Aryballoi. The one has a shoulder decoration, while the other is black with horizontal lines on the central upper part of the vessel. The first by character constitutes a continuation of the sub-Mycenaean Proto-Geometric tradition. Both types of

---

[12] Small vessels compared to the Attic and Argive vessels; see Coldstream 1977:172-3 in the chapter on Corinth and Western Greece.
[13] The beginning of this period, in the last quarter of the 8th century BC, depends on the researchers chronological definition; see the following pages and in the section on chronological tables.
[14] "Type-fossil" as it is called by Neeft.
[15] In general it should be noted that the findings at the Kerameikos graves in Athens provide an impressive and reliable cross section, however it must be added that many of the imported oriental vessels were found in isolated corners within the temple site complexes. In order to comprehensively examine the subject in various sectors and works, see Markoe 1985:117 n.142 for details on findings from north Syria and bronze relief works found in Greece, particularly in Olympia. See also Boardman 1985:69, fig. 53.

[16] See Amyx 1988 II: 436, on the distribution of Corinthian vessels and their influence in other places.
[17] Analysis of the Black-Figure Aryballoi with more detailed and richer evaluation will be done further on. It is rarely used as a model for the analysis and differentiation of Proto-Corinthian sub-Geometric vessels.
[18] Some researchers differentiate the term sub-Geometric from the black-figure Aryballoi, such as Neeft (1987:18, n 28, 29). According to Neeft the linear silhouettes provide an additional sub-division.
[19] See for example Coldstream (1977: 172-3, fig. 56a) and interesting to see is the bold pattern on the Oinochoe vessel from Cumae, which prominently combines the transition from harsh geometry to the flexibility of the early archaic or Early Proto-Corinthian period (EPC).

decoration, however, continue on into the Proto-Corinthian period and the second is particularly common to the globular Aryballoi or in other words: Early Proto-Corinthian (see illustration no. 2).

During the Geometric period the globular vessel had a small base, which was extended over time, often achieving a conical form but returning to its rotund globular shape. This trend is reinforced later during the Proto-Corinthian period. There are those, like Desborogh (see Neeft 1987:28, n. 57) who claim the vessel is a miniature, truncated type of the Lekythos that disappeared in Attica at the end of the Proto-Geometric period, as did the trifoliate Lekythos of the Geometric period. In terms of function, however, during the Geometric period the vessel was designed to contain various oils.

As said, the first phase of the Proto-Corinthian Aryballos decoration, the globular phase, resembles the sub-Mycenaean Proto-Geometric decoration: the shoulder decoration followed by the horizontal lines decoration on a black vessel.

In terms of form, during this period the globular vessels were given a wide stem, round body, a short cylindrical neck and a flat handle reaching from shoulder to rim (see tables on p. 48). The globular vessel is the smallest in size of the four types mentioned. The vessel became narrower and elongated, with a longer neck, a wide handle and a larger and thicker mouth. There are changes in size and in scale of decoration however, during the Proto-Corinthian globular period; however the opening of an additional frieze from the central decoration, other than the shoulder, is not necessarily a sign of chronology, i.e. of a later stage or any other stage in the decorative development process.[20]

Over time the decoration is also integrated into the vessel base. The combined well known ray motif appears gradually on the rim and from the base upwards, replacing the black color and horizontal lines. The final stage of the globular period integrates rays on the base (see decoration development chart on p. 13).[21]

A minimal decoration of animals continues to appear and to advance in its present expression with the birds and fish models being particularly prominent, as well as the plants, the rosettes motif and various decorative combinations. Most of the motifs seem to be taken from the Oriental lexicon (see illustrations on p. 15).[22] There is a development in the rosettes motif: it first appears with separate petals, which then become a single joined unit

creating, within the geometric tradition, a diamond like schematic motif. This unit is separated later to emphasize the base and leaves, by incision, a technique that continues and is probably acquired from the oriental form of decorating metal vessels.

It is important to note at this stage the symmetrical organization of the motifs, especially that of the figurative array: the heraldic groups, for example. These motifs develop and are boldly reinforced in later periods.
The practice of decorating the Aryballos body with a figurative frieze over maximum circumference of the vessel commenced during the globular period. It constitutes a continuation of the geometric tradition. With time the frieze expanded. The vessel stem remains in accordance with the vessel's function and its varying size and shape (over 70 mm). When the vessel is smaller it is flattened with an almost flat shoulder and low stem. During the conical shape period of the vessel the stem is still wide but narrows down as the vessel approaches its ovoid shape. During the ovoid shape period, decorative subjects and method elements from the Geometric period remain: the vessel shoulder serves as the central decorative area and most of the vessel is decorated with black horizontal lines. The familiar checkers stripe under the shoulder also remains (from the Proto-Geometric tradition).

On the other hand, the decorative rays that commenced during the globular period, continue to develop. At first they appear as a continuation of the expression characteristic of the sub-Mycenaean Proto-Geometric period. Later it stops, and reappears influenced by the Black Figure geometric Aryballoi design. In any event, at this stage it adheres to the familiar angular geometric decorative scheme (see illustration no. 1).[23]

Illustration no. 1
Bird Plant Group decoration on shoulder
(Neeft 1987:fig 16)

There is no doubt that the oriental style rays decoration dominated and most certainly complied with the needs of the local artist in search of such a prominent formative element to continue the geometric tradition but in sophisticated form (to be elaborated further on). The other floral motifs, the various fillings in decorative combinations and the figurative motifs that develop,

---

[20] According to Neeft 1987:37, 49, 60 and contrary to Coldstream; at a later stage this change characterizes a periodical development.
[21] Especially in the Bird Plant Group. See Neeft 1987:82. The motif integrates nicely during the conical vessel period. See later about the ray motif.
[22] More of this in the summary chapter; and for instance concerning the identity of the birds or roosters that are common at this stage, researched by those that regard the motifs as being of pure Oriental source, for example see Boardman 1985: 76 or Neeft 1987:n.206.

---

[23] The origins of the Mycenaean and sub-Mycenaean stage should be mentioned as these will be dealt with concerning the development and progression of the motif in general. In addition this stage has reciprocal implications and influences on all matters pertaining to the transfer of motifs (from the east to the Aegean world and vice versa) as will be seen in the following. For a detailed examination of the subject see Crowly 1989.

integrate with heraldic or other symmetry, all of which coincide with the artist's new challenges.

During the vessel's conical period, the decorative friezes increased to cover the entire body. The rays replace the black expanse, departing from the stem upwards. The shoulder strip in many cases empties and the decoration, including the strips, transfers to the body. The change in decorative tradition transfers to the ovoid period, the stem and base become wider or narrower depending on vessel size. During its ovoid period, the Aryballos is no longer so small (relatively, from 70 to 100 mm[24]) and this trend continues, that is to say, the production of larger vessels.

The transition from conical form to the ovoid vessel allowed artists to incorporate new decorative elements. Decorations became more interesting and the change in size attracted additional artists and potters. The sub-Mycenaean Proto-Geometric traditions continued with the appearance of these new motifs, even up until the piriform, pointed shape stage. The shoulders show a popular repetitive frieze of dogs bending or in motion (three in number or later two) duplicating the frieze on the vessel body. The geometric horizontal stripes continue to appear (see illustration no. 2).

Illustration no. 2
The piriform Aryballos
(Koukia type, Neeft 1987:155).

At the piriform stage (as diagnosed by Johansen 1923:161), the ovoid body becomes pointed towards the base; the vessel is higher and has a wider stem.

New decorative motifs appear such as the scale pattern (illustration no. 3). The rays have taken on palmette formation; some are highlighted by incision, spreading from the base upwards, and likewise on the shoulder. All these constitute copies or local adaptations of typical Oriental floral decorations.[25] The traditional checkers decoration (illustration no. 3) continues alongside these, being combined up until the early Corinthian period (approx. 625-600 BC, see tables p. 48).

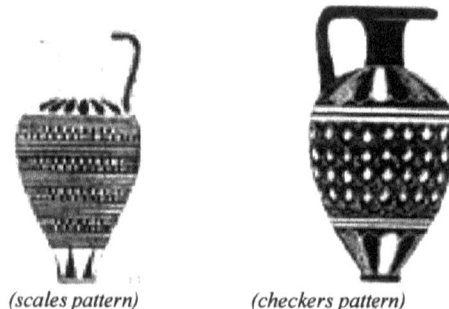

| (scales pattern) | (checkers pattern) |

Illustration no. 3
The piriform Aryballoi
(Neeft 1987:274).

A.2 THE CORINTHIAN PERIOD

Throughout this entire period, i.e. from the Late Proto-Corinthian (LPC) period until the Late Corinthian (LC) period, around 650-550 BC, there are two principle dominant shape types of Aryballoi: the round shaped Aryballos and the flat bottomed Aryballos.[26]

The round Aryballos (see illustrations p. 15) originated in the LPC period, as the Orientalizing era intensified. It is not common and in fact is very rarely found prior to the Early Corinthian (EC) period, around 625-600 BC, during which period the vessel was very common. Later, during the Middle Corinthian (MC) period, around 600-575 BC, the vessel dwindles, and finally, during the first Late Corinthian period (LC-I, around 575-550 BC) it becomes quite rare.

The round Aryballoi from the EC period were generally used as grave offerings.[27] They are common, as said, but at the same time were of good quality in terms of material and decoration. Three principle motifs appear on these vessels: the Padded Dancers motif, the Marching Hoplites motif and the Quatre Foil pattern motif, an Oriental motif of Assyrian origin (see Amyx 1988 II:647) usually designed to fill in spaces.[28]

During the MC period the vessel increases in size and breadth. It is characterized by decorations of the scales pattern group. During this period a more stereotypical approach was taken for decorations, along with mass production of the vessels accompanied by a deterioration in quality. In terms of use: it is possible that the flat bottomed Aryballos replaced the round due to functionality, in other words, functionality dictated the size and shape. The desire to produce a more balanced

---

[24] See discussion Neeft 1987: 271-2 concerning classification of vessels according to size and shape during this period and during the piriform shape period, and according to decorative subject concerning the opinions of the various researchers (Johansen 1923:161, Payne 1931:478-9, Dunbabin 1962:ad. no. 45)

[25] See for example Boardman 1985:74-81, fig. 26 c-d, regarding the dominant use of Oriental motifs in decorating during this period and floral designs in particular such as the lotus and palmette.

[26] Two other, less common, types that also appear are: the double-walled round vessel, most probably designed as tableware for two spices (Amyx 1988, Vol. III:443-4) and the round vessel with the plaster decorated head that served as a handle. These vessels have some affinity to the Pyxis with the decorative head or the female protome handles. In any event, these are properly expressed in the works of the boar-Hunt painter (Amyx 1988:Cat.163f, 314).

[27] As during the following period, and see Payne 1931 in general and Amyx 1988 III:442 in particular

[28] Began its journey in Mesopotamian art as a simplified rosette. See about its progression in the East and the Aegean world Crowly 1989:91.

vessel led to the development of a base or flat bottom, and to the onset of producing larger vessels.[29]

The flat bottomed Aryballoi appear mainly during the 6th century BC. These vessels originate in the EC period, during which they were smaller, more globular and with a narrow stem. Most have scale and palmette decorations, reminiscent of the Proto-Corinthian piriform Aryballoi decorations. Patterns with decorative figures are rare during this period.

The characteristic vessel that appears during the MC period is larger with a wider base. The vessel, as said, is reliably represented within the scale pattern group and especially the works of the painter known as the Scale Painter. Additional beautiful patterns come from the Chimera Group potters house and from renowned painters such as the Painter of Louvre, the Painter of Berlin F 1090, as well as the Otterlo Painter and the Laurion Painter.[30]

Figurative decoration continues during the LC-I period, a period that maintains the traditional styles of the MC period however with a dull monotonous expression and less quality. During this period the outstanding artist is that known as the Herzegovina Painter, along with others such as the Torino Painter and the artist known as the Winged Lion Painter. Compared to other vessels of this period, such as those with coating or the red background (LC-I red ground) that show a breakthrough or renaissance of artistic expression – these Aryballoi are of poor artistic expression and in fact constitute a terminal form of production (Amyx 1988 III:445).

For a deeper and more thorough understanding of the subject we shall move on to an artistic analysis of painting development in Corinthian vessels for the periods aforementioned. The analysis will focus on the various Aryballoi and will deal with their connections to other vessels within a local contest, a discussion and analysis of complementary findings (to the research subject) and comparative parallels from other sites.

A.3 DEVELOPMENT OF THE STYLE AND DECORATIVE SUBJECT IN THE CORINTHIAN ARYBALLOI – AN ARTISTIC ANALYSIS (See tables on pp. 13-15)

During the Geometric period decorations on Corinthian pottery are simple and restricted compared to parallel Attic ceramic expression. Other than birds, there is a dull description of figures (see for example Coldstream 1968:16-20).

Within framework of Corinthian decoration, Attic ceramics by comparison are adorned with a rich repertoire of decorative content and subjects including the figurative motifs and the narrative fashion in which they are revealed, especially during the late Geometric period. It is therefore necessary to understand how the Corinthian artists eagerly transitioned to the Orientalizing stage and to the new and exciting implementation of their artistic expression, which most probably commenced during the first quarter of the 8th century BC.[31]

There is no doubt that the widespread trading, with activities initiated by local Corinthians and reciprocally with external entities from the east, such as the Phoenicians, added change and daring to the spirit of creation and the search for new forms. It should be mentioned that the transfer of goods from place to place also entails the transfer of functional objects including art objects that were given local attribution and assimilation and were later marketed throughout the region and even exported outside of local territories overseas, to other areas of consumption. The continuous passage between the various colonies and trade stations no doubt formed a complex system of absorbing various artistic elements that appeared in their original form or progressed and changed.[32] This was in fact the most significant turnabout, which will be discussed in the following pages.

Therefore, alongside the transition of motifs from the geometric decorative traditions to the Proto-Corinthian period, as we have seen, a relatively early abandonment occurred of the general geometric style decorative framework. Friction with oriental motifs was a catalyst for constructing richer artistic patterns, which gave a push to experimenting with the creation of additional variations, with a curved as opposed to angular outline, suitable for the construction of narrative topics that require richer descriptivism. This was true for both painters and potters, expressed in the vessel design. The skilled hands of the local potters accepted willingly and perhaps even enthusiastically, the possibility of adding new elements close to their hearts. These elements served as a richer and more integral basis with the painters (themselves or others).

The art of incision, adopted from the metalwork decorations of oriental vessels, such as metal plates, as will be shown on the following pages, led to a breakthrough that enabled the refinement of silhouette figures filled with internal details. This new expression took on form of the Black-Figure Style.

Painting on Proto-Corinthian ceramics is based, as said, on specialized miniature expression on small vessels. There were several Proto-Corinthian artists with a more

---

[29] See Seeberg 1971:9f. This most probably concerns a new model of vessel and not the renewal of the known early Proto-Corinthian "Aryballe pansu".

[30] A general discussion of these artists by Payne 1931, 1933 and the reference Amyx 1988 III:444. A remarkable Aryballos in this period from this group of artists is known as Basel Hydra Aryballos – with a unique and singular narrative topic decoration. See Amyx 1988: Cat.180f, Pl 67.

[31] See Boardman 1985:77-78 and Benson 1995. For the historical background from whence this infrastructure emerged, see also Salmon 1984.

[32] Or were added to existing systems and changed, or forgotten, reappeared and even returned to the east. For example from Cyprus, see article on the ritual vessel, Stern 1994.

monumental expression, however still small compared to the Attic amphora of the time (mid 7th century BC), such as the famous Chigi Ople or those painted by the painter known as the Hound Painter.[33] In any event, the Aryballoi served as the first and most characteristic vessels of the first stages of the EC period (also known as the Orientalizing period or the period of oriental influence). The first signs of Orientalizing in Corinth probably appeared during the Early Proto-Corinthian period (EPC) on the small globular flat based Aryballoi (the "Aryballe pansu" according to Johansen).

The figurative decoration appears together with conventional and floral motifs and is expressed in the outline technique, which was divided into two groups: the first group (Plate 1:1-2) includes the small Aryballos (from Boston) that depicts birds on a linear surface with rosettes that fill in the space. They are hand painted naturally with imprecision especially the petals description! Another description that appears on the Aryballos (from Naples, Plate 1:2) includes other animals, such as a fish, a rooter, and decorative elements that fill in the space.

The second group depicts a four legged animal, probably a deer such as the one on the Aryballos of Syracuse (Plate 1:4) with two friezes containing figurative elements. The shoulder shows a hound chasing a rabbit: an early narrative that becomes popular in Proto-Corinthian vessel paintings. Another Aryballos (from Naples, Plate 1:4, 5) shows a similar, more refined expression of an animal, probably a deer (gazelle or goat?) placed in a frieze on a surface of horizontal lines positioned higher in terms of the artist's division of space, with the rays motif (higher than usual) supporting from below.

In between these two groups there is an outstanding Aryballos (Plate 1:7, 8 in the British Museum) known as the Evelyn Painter Aryballos. The shoulder shows a rich composition: a set of birds, rosettes, stars and triangles filling in the space "crosswise" and symmetrically organized around a rolled spiral tree formed decoration. The central frieze on the vessel body is divided into sections by more sophisticated cylindrical combinations, and on the one side probably describes a deer hunt, the spotted body turned aside facing a threatening dog, and in the background a large flying bird.[34]

On the other side rides the hunter(?) on a horse followed by an armed soldier. A large water bird completes this group array which faces one of the cylindrical plants combinations (see for comparison Johansen 1923:59, figs. 34-39).[35]

In this frieze, as in the previous examples, old and new motifs combine: space is filled with early geometric and sub-geometric motifs and the use of new and strange asymmetric motifs. It is dominated by the outline technique. The horse silhouette and the spotted deer with conical blots are an expression of the early renowned Black Figure painting technique.

At a later stage of this period (EPC) there is a good example, characterizing the development of the painter known as The Bird-Protome Painter (Plate 1:3), and at a later stage of the painter known as The Painter of the Hopping Birds (Plate 1:6). This last vessel is decorated with horizontal lines while the shoulder has a frieze of young birds nesting painted in the black-figure technique. It would appear that this stage commenced the "Black-Figures" style, known as the First Middle Proto-Corinthian period (MPC-I).[36]

The work of the artist known as the Corneto Painter (Plate 1:11-13) constitutes an interesting additional stage in the progression of the artists that paint the Aryballoi.[37] The artist specializes in painting on the specific vessel and the central frieze has an interesting and more varied description of animals such as a bull, goat, deer, lion or panther, as well as a combination of a person standing between the beasts as well as a motif of wild animals attacking a calf, a repetitive motif in paintings of the Archaic period (Amyx 1988, Vol. II, 376, n.11).

In face of the progress in decorative quality or the advanced change in its expression, particularly of animals, it is interesting whether these motifs of lions or other wild animals attacking herd of cattle, were from scenes the artist had seen in nature or were a copy of oriental motifs, or a combination of both. In other words, the wild-animals motif from the east was used as an element for constructing a scene of local character?! It can be assumed, in any event, that the inspirational model came from the east. The skill for painting these motifs on such small vessels has since moved to a very advanced artistic stage, sophisticated locally.

During the following period (MPC-II) significant development occurred in presentation of the varied decorative elements and subjects, based on widespread use of the black-figure technique. In the works of two well known painters - the Huntsmen Painter and the Ajax painter, who specialized in painting Aryballoi, stylish innovations emerge displaying excellent skill and daring with richer narrative expression.

The Ajax Painter describes mythological scenes on some of his vessels.[38] The central upper frieze on the Aryballos

---

[33] See Amyx 1988: Cat 32, 301 no. A-3, despite the Olpe vessel, the decoration itself is also miniature. For the Hound Painter see Amyx 1988: Cat.26-28,301, and for Attic vessels, see for example: Cook 1972:Pl. 16 for the expression on the vessel known as Nessos Amphora.

[34] Is this a primordial phase or renaissance of the local narrative scene or a direct copy of a foreign model? More about this further on.

[35] See also Plate 2:48. Boardman regards the cylindrical plants combination as the **tree of life** in a stylish oriental format Boardman 1975:40, fig 34 and see the subject on p. 22.

[36] As in larger vessels such as the Oinochoe: in the Cumae Group, see Amyx 1988 Pl 3:1a-b or the Oinochoe of Syracuse with the strange monstrous figure, same Pl 4:1.

[37] Some attribute it to the famous Toulouse Painter, see Dunbabin 1953: 176.

[38] More about this painter's work associated with the issue of borrowing oriental motifs (Cypro-Phoenician), see on the chapter dealing with Aryballoi and plates – Phoenician metal bowls.

(of Berlin, Plate 1:9,10) is an apparently **primal description** of Ajax suicide scene.[39]

The suicide scene of Ajax.
(Detail from the Aryballos on plate 1:10)

This scene fascinated Corinthian artists: the hero is lying on his left side, his left hand is holding a sword and his right arm is bent at the elbow across his chest.
In presenting the motif the beginning of focusing on well known mythological scenes is obvious: other figures do not belong to the scene. The unification of figures to one scene in the frieze is not yet of interest to the Corinthian artist, or because the subject had not yet captured the proper focus.

On other Aryballoi such as this last one there is another common scene: the lion attacking one of the hunters. The subject is described on a vessel known as the Chigi Vase.[40] Towards the end of the 7th century BC, use of this scene dwindles and diminishes, except perhaps in the west (Etruria), where it continued with an advanced version (probably local or archaic Etrusco-Corinthian).[41] On the back of one of these vessels, with this motif, there is a winged figure holding a snake and a bird in his hands. This may be the figure of the Master of Animals, as proposed by Amyx (1988, Vol. II, 367), however there is no doubt that the hunting scenes and the winged figure openly depict a local expression of common oriental motifs. These motifs permeate the local framework of artistic expression at its beginning and in fact constitute the onset of implementing local scenes that combine episodes of Greek mythology. The subject of Ajax, in this case, serves as one of the initial and uniquely prominent characteristics. It appears together with other oriental motifs.

During this period the figures on the Proto-Corinthian Aryballoi are described on additional stripes outside of the central frieze. The vessel expressed by the Ajax painter or by the Huntsmen Painter becomes more elongated and pointed.

The Huntsmen Painter specializes in describing hunting scenes in the friezes, scenes that describe short people with large pointed beards and long hair with thick prominent thighs, fighting and hunting animals with flexible spears that wave through the air (Plate 2:3,4). The Aryballos shows three hunters assisting a bull being attacked by two lions. This type of scene is typical of the Corneto Painter as well. Attention should be given to the flight of the bird on the right that fills the background, a common oriental motif (perhaps in its Egyptian format).

The bottom frieze shows a scene of dogs chasing a rabbit fleeing straight into the net trap (an undoubtedly interesting innovation) in the scene's common motif, characteristic of secondary friezes on Proto-Corinthian vases.

Hunting topics are common amongst the painters of that period. In one scene (from a Syracuse Aryballos, Amyx 1988:Cat. 24, no. a-1), among other subjects, a deer stands before a seated Griffin. The seated Griffin motif, which receives its legitimacy and unique style during this period, is probably taken from the reservoire of motifs common to the oriental world.[42]

It should also be noted that at this stage, the second stage of the MPC period, which continued until the mid 7th century BC, a new type of painting began that bridged between this and the later period: the monumental painting alongside the miniature painting. Painters such as the Hound Painter, by improving the technique with incised lines in order to depict anatomical details, work on larger vessels. Use of the **Black Polychrome** technique with delicate incision and with added color (red, white, yellow, and see below), rendered a unique result that is reminiscent, even more than the incision style that characterizes the "Black Figure", of the delicate oriental incision on various metal vessels[43] (here on the Olpe vessel, see plate 2:5).

The visual novelty of the black polychrome Proto-Corinthian technique was expressed mainly in the engraving of figures or patterns over the black glazed surface of the vessel with a combined emphasis of details (incised) using purplish red, yellow and white colors. This phenomenon is preeminent in a group of vessels

---

[39] Dated 700-675 BC. See Payne 1931:137, Benson 1995a:343-44, fig.20.12a and recently in an interesting article on the beginning of the appearance of the specific motifs or scenes through their expression in Greek art, Jenkins 2002:154, that brings an earlier example (despite the chronological difficulty) from metal art (bronze) in the Geometric period (the last quarter of the 8th century BC) in Greece.

[40] On the Olpe frieze and for instance see Benson 1953: 18-19 or Boardman 2002:32.

[41] The human figure (the hunter) is almost entirely devoured: its feet peep out of the lion's mouth. This subject is quite common and appears on bucchero vessels where the decoration is emphasized with engraving, and on Etrusco-Corinthian vessels. On several vessels (at Villa Giulia in Rome and the Louvre Museum, see Payne 1931) see Amyx 1988:II 367.

[42] See Bisi 1965:22-106 and also Crowly 1989:52, on the Minoan and Mycenaean griffin iconography as said, Tamvaki 1974. See for comparison a unique work and rare description of griffins during a deer hunt on an Athenian pyxis, a Mycenaean carving, see Immerwahr 1971: Pl. 32, 106-7. Also peruse the interesting (and old) essay by Frankfort on characteristics of the Cretan griffin, Frankfort 1936-7.

[43] Which is combined integrally to the surface of the black glazed vessel, as expressed in the metal vessels, whereas in the Black-Figure style emphasis is mainly on the outlines upon a different background (and of course together with engraving to describe the internal details). The characteristic engraving originating from metal vessels and ivory works in the east, see Payne 1931:7, Beazley 1952:1 ("The Road to Black-Figure"), Boardman 1974:9, Amyx 1988:364, Cook:1997:45.

known as the Chigi group and at its center the Chigi painter. This technique is very significant with proven influence over other potteries (especially in Etruria).[44]

The scattered findings undoubtedly testify to the dominance of Corinth as the initial and major originator and as the number one production center of vessels in this technique.[45] The decorative compositions associated with this technique are no different from the others and the figurative images are usually of animals while the patterns are rosettes, scales patterns[46] and tongues as well as stripes that are separate or combined or in concentric circles painted over the surface of the black glazed vessel. The impetus, which commenced as said during the MPC period (more precisely – MPC-II), reached its peak during the LPC and dwindled during the transitional period (TR) with its qualities flawed. It did not survive the transition over to massive production the result of international trading requirements on the one hand and local demand on the other.

During the LPC period the impetus continued and achieved new heights with a rich and complex style (known by Johansen as the Style Magnifique) which combines technical precision and almost perfect painting. On tiny vessels such as the Aryballoi, the artist's skilled precision flourished. The flourishing artists of this period are the artists known as: the Chigi Painter (known also as the Macmillan Painter), the Boston Painter and the Sacrifice Painter.[47]

The Aryballos known as the Macmillan Aryballos (at the British Museum) is a piriform vessel, dominantly unique (Plate 2:6) especially its top, plastic part designed as a lion head. There are other examples of plastic design of elements such as these in another Aryballos (of Berlin and see Amyx 1988:370) in which, alongside the head, there are Daedalic style masks[48] and the vertical handle made in the shape of a crouching lion.

The decoration on this vessel is a marvelously skilled and precise work of art: above the central frieze, on the shoulder, there is a floral chain and characteristic rays spread out from the base. The central frieze depicts warriors during battle and underneath there is an additional frieze describing a rabbit hunt, a chariot race

and animal and monster figures. Despite the minute dimensions, the technical precision and the artistic level are of the highest quality.

The black polychrome technique is flourishing (combined with the Black Figures technique[49] and the black glaze) and this impressive expression moves from the Aryballoi to Pyxides, Olpai and Oinochoai and other vessels and flourishes everywhere.

The painter known as The Boston Painter (see illustrations no. 4a-b and plate 2:7) refined the floral combination patterns. The animal and monster figures in the central frieze are presented as individual units with no affinity. The combinations and attributes that appear inside the actual figures are especially interesting, such as the winged and bearded figure facing right in a set for running position or the lion with a bearded head emerging from its back[50] and the warrior with a typical shield that has a panther behind him in profile with its head facing the front (probably in order to distinguish differences between it and the lion. For more about the lion figure derived from neo-Hittite art and additional oriental motifs, see Appendix 1 on p. 45). The sophistication, the skill and the use of many motifs taken from the oriental lexicon are characteristic of the period, although they are not always presented with such rich detail.

Illustration no. 4a
The central frieze on the Aryballos by the Boston Painter
(Amyx 1988: Cat, Pl. 11:2b)

24 (a) From a Protocorinthian vase;
(b) Stone relief from Carchemish.

Illustration no. 4b
Comparison of the motif to a neo-Hittite relief
(Boardman 1985:76, fig. 24a-b)

There are painters that specialize in certain subjects and their way of expression becomes very special, such as the

---

[44] See the work by Manchester 1991 on this unique Proto-Corinthian technique that emerged in the mid 7th century BC.
[45] First see Payne 1931:18-19 and especially the comprehensive report: Weinberg 1943, Amyx (& Lawrence) 1975, Stoops 1977-1978, Stillwell (& Benson) 1984 and in CVA Vol. 13. For other sites in Greece (such as Kerameikos, Perachora), the islands (Ithaca and Rhodes) and in the west like in Italy: Pithekoussai, Taranto and others and in Sicily (Gela, Catania) see Amyx 1988:676-7
[46] See mainly Neeft 1987:277-281 who assembled over 100 vessels with this pattern (Scale Pattern, see illustration 3), a pattern characteristic of vessel expression using the black polychrome technique. Neeft divided them into sub groups according to shape and decoration.
[47] Known by this name because of the ritual scene of sacrificing an ox on an Aegean Oinochoe fragment; however the expression is identical in the beautiful descriptions on the Aryballoi. See Amyx 1988: Cat 35 no. A-1, Pl 12:1a-b; Vol. II:370-71.
[48] In itself of great significance, and see Appendix 3 "The Deadalic Phenomenon" on pp. 46-47.

[49] See Amyx 1988:540 for the history of this technique and its complex integration with Black-Figure friezes.
[50] For this context see Boardman 1985:76 concerning the inspiration of oriental motifs and especially lions (illustration 4b and in the summary)

one known as Head in the Air Painter, who creates the animal figure described in an upright position with a protruding head (Plate 3:1-3), suggesting animal pride and arrogance characteristic of most of the animals he painted. There may have been a direct connection or even emotional affinity between the painter and these animals; in any event, an acquaintance of some sort is almost absolute when expressed so uniquely. This painter may have been copying from some source and used his brilliant imagination. It seems more probable that in presentation of such expression the artist had to have developed a personal affinity to animals.[51] At another workshop, works of the painter known as The Torr Painter develop a style that is no less sensitive in depicting animals (Plate 3:4-6). It is interesting to observe how the painter breaks through boundaries very gracefully presenting the figure of a rabbit, in the bottom frieze, standing on its hind legs with its head protruding from the top surface thereby creating dimensions and connection between the subjects. Notice the familiar and common rosette pattern that fills in the background. Many motifs and especially the various animal and monster descriptions, characteristic of many vessels, seem to have become a first class Corinthian expertise.

The TR period, which bridges between the LPC period and the EC period at around 630-615 BC (as defined by Payne 1931:28-34, and see chronological tables), has no greater importance but rather is a continuous process based on another stage in the accelerated development of ceramic material in Corinth. There are changes in the background patterns such as the rosettes: the axle wheel, characteristic of the LPC period becomes a bunch of rosettes with incision for emphasis, giving the petals more dominant expression. The battle scenes, the races and the hunts gradually disappear replaced with more and more friezes of animals and mythological beasts in conventional poses. Sphinxes and sirens appear alongside panthers, lions and birds (predominantly on small vessels), etc. There are also heraldic groups of animals, especially on the Alabstra vessels, surrounding a central motif. The hunting scenes that include human figures as well as the "dogs chasing rabbits into a net trap" motif continue to appear on the bottom frieze of the Aryballoi.

Prominent painters are: The Griffin Painter, who specializes in the common scenes presenting animals such as a swan or snake in between two seated sphinxes or griffins, and The Painter of Palermo 489 and The Sphinx Painter, who generally express themselves on larger vessels. All have a great influence during this bridging period.

The EC period (approx. 620/25-590 BC) has great significance in the development of the Aryballoi. Payne (1931:43-57) refers to the period as "The Early Corinthian Orientalizing Style", and at the time of defining this title attached the element of Orientalizing to Corinth, perhaps thereby indicating the beginning of dominant oriental influence in Corinth. In fact, according to all the previous data mentioned, the Orientalizing stage was in full swing. During this period, despite the abundance of material and the mass production of vessels, there is also an obvious expression of impressive personal skill among the various artists.

During this period the greatest numbers of Corinthian ceramic vessels were the Aryballoi. The Round Aryballoi as well as the Alabastra vessels and especially the Sack-shaped Alabastron which become vessels heavily consumed and in demand. These vessels have become common in the Mediterranean world. The distribution is directly attributed to demand for the specific vessel because of its function in containing perfumed oils. The important production center was in Corinth.[52]

The uniqueness of the vessel was not only measured by its functionality but by its fine quality ceramic and art work. The painters whose work dominates this period were: The Painter from Palermo 489, mentioned earlier in the TR period, and his follower the Columbus Painter, as well as the one known as The Duel Painter (plate 4:1-4), who presents his work on a large and complex group of round Aryballoi in a style characterized by the motif of a warrior dueling another warrior, facing him. The integration of a narrative subject with a conventional one with appearance of the warriors and of other figures (usually animals and monsters) and a dominant background filling pattern such as rosettes, are characteristic of the period.

An additional motif or group is the Padded Dancers group (plate 4:10), significantly appearing on the Aryballoi and Alabastra vessels.[53] Some appear sloppy and even decadent however there are painters, such as the one known as the Welcome Painter, who succeeded in illustrating a graceful and amusing expression with these figures.

Combining the dancers with other images, such as sirens, is not necessarily a narrative; however, in technical terms, adaptation of these figures to each other in an amusing composition is interesting.

A prominent painter, such as the Duel Painter, expressed himself on large and small (Aryballoi) vessels and was also known as: The Heraldic Lions Painter because his painting on the round Aryballos describes a pair of seated lions in a heraldic array.[54] In this style and its

---

[51] A similar and somewhat later expression can be discerned in the works of the painter known as The Painter of the Frankfurt Olpe who expressed this unique element with great talent but on a larger vessel, see Amyx 1988:Cat.Pl.16,1.

[52] On the subject and the trail of perfume manufacture, see Amyx 1988 Vol. II:375, n. 21.

[53] See in the following on this subject of the described group and of the associated significances in relation to another focal motif: the figure of the goddess Artemis/Potnia Theron.

[54] A distinctive oriental motif. As for the lion, the development of the mane is of interest: the initial model was a flame-like pattern similar to the Assyrian model, and as seen in the well known Chigi Olpe vessel or in early works by the painter known as Palermo 489, and see Amyx 1988 II:663, cat.58: A1, A2. Later the mane is given a more standardized, square shape or an expression of sloped crisscross

characteristic expression that continues on even into the MC period (around 595-570 BC) with other painters, most of the vessel surface is decorated with one large scene or motif (Plate 4:5-9) that faithfully emphasizes the features of the rounded vessel: the round vessel with the large flat base and especially that with the flat bottom.

During this period there is greater use of larger vessels such as the vessel used for mixing wine, the Corinthian Krater, also known as the Column Krater. A frieze depicting a group of warriors is also characteristic of large vessels, as are well known mythological scenes characteristic of the period, such as the suicide of Ajax or Heracles dining with Eurytos, king of Thessaly, his daughter and sons, which appears on the famous Eurythios Krater (from the Louvre). The subject narrative is not cancelled this time by the indefinite inclusion of animals in the composition.

During the Mid Corinthian period and the following Late period (around 570-550 BC), there is a variety of known styles but there is no prominent style breakthrough. A repeated style is that of the Scale Pattern, mentioned earlier. Use of the Aryballos vessel decreases, the quality of decoration deteriorates and becomes crude and inexact.[55]

---

squares, or is simply painted red. For the integration of the oriental lion motif into Greece see also Boardman 1985:75-6, fig. 23.

[55] It is interesting that by comparison, on the Pyxides of the parallel period there are detailed and precise descriptions of archaic scenes with a traditional oriental character (animals and monsters) together with famous epic scenes. See Pemberton 1989:Pl.26 Figs. 251,253 concerning the ceramic material in the Demeter and Kore temples at Corinth.

**A.4 DEVELOPMENT OF STYLE AND DECORATIVE
SUBJECT IN THE ARYBALLOS – THE PROTO-
CORINTHIAN PERIOD: SUMMARY TABLE**

1. The geometric stage Aryballos

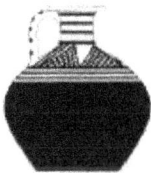

*The sub-Mycenaean/Proto-Geometric style
by tradition*

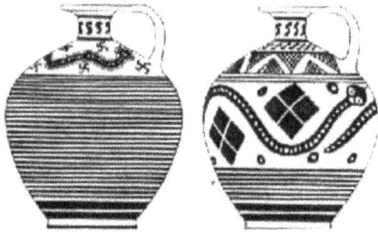

2. The globular stage Aryballoi by the geometrical tradition (a),

at the motifs absorption and introduction stage

and the integration of the new, oriental type elements (b)

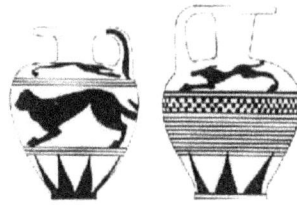

*3. Decorations on conical Aryballoi
(Illustrations: Amyx 1988, 1996, Neeft 1987)*

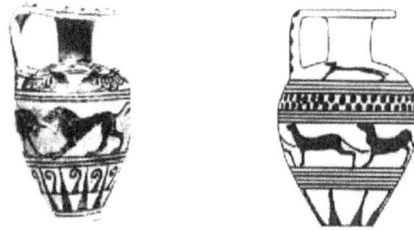

4. The ovoid

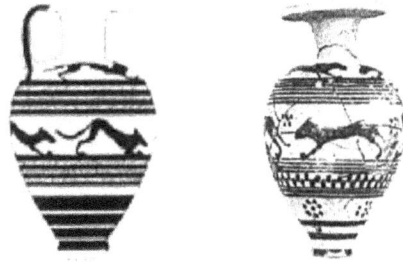

5. The pointed

**DEVELOPMENT OF THE DECORATIVE STYLE AND
SUBJECT – THE CORINTHIAN PERIOD: SUMMARY
TABLE**
(Illustrations: Payne 1931, Amyx 1988, Pemberton 1989)

Vessel from the MC period and a common frieze

LPC
↓

MC - common motifs and patterns outside of the central frieze

EC

MC

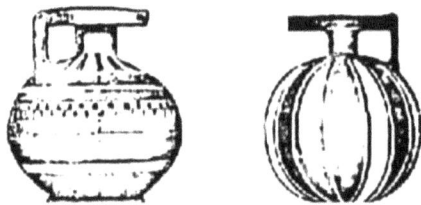

EC (less common types)

The total variety is characteristic of the Corinthian period.
Decoration during the LC is sloppy.

ABSORPTION OF THE ORIENTAL MOTIF AND ITS DEVELOPMENT WITHIN FRAMEWORK OF THE COMMON ARCHAIC FRIEZE

Transitional

EPC

EC

MPC

MC

LPC

LC
(Illustrations: Payne 1931, Amyx 1988)

LPC

There is obvious rigidity in style during the stages of absorbing and integrating the geometric tradition style. Later there began a gradual refining and control of anatomical knowledge and of controlled shading that peaked during the transitional stage and the Early Corinthian period.

Within this framework of Corinthian vase painting development we are particularly interested in two characteristic subjects of scenes that decorate the vessels: the Potnia Theron/Artemis figure and the groups of dancers motif, which includes the motif of the "Padded Dancers".

A.5 THE POTNIA THERON/ARTEMIS MOTIF AND ACCOMPANYING MOTIFS: A REPRESENTATIVE ICONOGRAPHY SUBJECT

Vase painting in the Archaic period in Corinth did not include prolific representation of Greek gods and goddesses as did the vase painting in the Attic material. On the other hand, the motif of the goddess as the mistress of animals, usually winged and holding animals in her hands, usually birds (Illustration no. 5) is relatively common to the Paintings on Corinthian vessels.

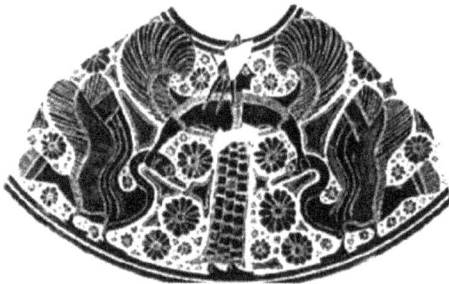

Illustration no. 5
Potnia Theron/Artemis holding birds by their necks (water birds) in a frieze decorating an Alabastron from the EC period
(Amyx 1988: Cat. Pl 41, 1)

THE EARLY MOTIF

The fact that the basic shape depicting the goddess remains consistent and almost unchanging, despite the changes in style and quality of expression in general, led researchers to the opinion that there was an early prototype upon which these were based and used over time. Some proposed the metope painting of a certain temple (Harlow 1977:31).

Other origins can serve as the source of the motif, such as the ivories in Ugarit (Schaffer 1939, 1949) that integrate local character with foreign influences, mainly Egyptian or a "Proto-Phoenician" blend, as seen by Barnett (1982:29), that imply the future of later periods, and particularly the 8th-6th centuries BC.

Signs indicating the Ugarit connection with the Aegean world are presented in the Pyxis cover from Minat al-Bayda, the port of Ugarit (14th century BC, Illustration no. 6), which describes a bare breasted goddess leaning on an altar or rock, holding a sheaf of wheat and flanked by two upright goats. The symmetry and composition are of Mesopotamian and Syrian style characteristic of the goddess Potnia Theron mastering animals' presentation. At the same time, the artist's work in depicting the woman excels in Mycenaean style features with details

from Minoan art such as the hairstyle, the cap she is wearing, her dress and bare breasts. This combination is interesting and gives rise for comparison due to the early integration of components characteristic of the two earlier sources from the Orient and from the Minoan and Mycenaean world.[56]

Illustration no. 6.
The Goddess Mastering the Animals,
on the Pyxis cover from Minat al-Bayda
(Moscati 1988:35)

This unique motif is rooted in the beginning of Mesopotamian art (see Plate 6:1, a seal from Susa – Uruk period – see Crowly 1989:34, 416), which is characterized already at an early stage by presenting the holding figure as a mark of control over animals but with no struggle.

Samples of this type in the form of the goddess Ishtar, the goddess of war Ianna-Ishtar, were found in Mari.[57] During the late Bronze Age, in addition to other details that characterize the figure (the wings, the spear, and sometimes the helmet) appearing in Mitannic and North Syrian regions - lions, goats, oxen, Ibexes and snakes appear alongside.[58]

---

[56] On the combination of styles and mainly the examination of the Late Mycenaean expression within the Syrian composition with its Mesopotamian features, see Barnett 1982:31-31(Ras Shamra), Pl. 24 (b) and Crowly 1989:34-39 for Mitannic-Syrian, Mesopotamian and Aegean precedents of the Potnia Theron motif that appears in this sample. Also the possible transition to Cyprus between the 16th-14th centuries BC (Crowly 1989:35 no.78). The goddess figure replaces the traditional Ishtar.

[57] Barrelet 1955:22-60, describes the items of clothing and other characteristics of Ianna-Ishtar and refers to the problems associated with finding the origins of this motif.

[58] Recounted mainly by Crowly 1989:Ch. 1: "Artistic Tradition and Iconographical Analysis" and ibid. on the international aspect, i.e. the integration with the Aegean region, Ch. 10: "The Aegean and the East, Artistic Heritage".

Presentation of several examples in plates, particularly on carved cylindrical seals, are excellent illustrates of the early stages that represent the motif:
Plate 5:6 – A Mitannic cylindrical seal.[59] The figure overcomes two sphinxes and grasps them from their hind legs.

Plate 6:3 – a Cyprian seal: the attire, the wings and the spear of Ishtar, the pointed horn shaped helmet is missing.

The appearance of the goddess is emphasized here and it possibly indicates the goddess mistress of the animals motif having moved to Cyprus from the Mesopotamian regions in the 16-14th centuries BC, where the goddess still appears in the form of Ishtar in the oriental form: the attire, wings and spear, except, as said, for the hat and helmet, with two sphinxes alongside.

Plate 6:4 – ivory from Ugarit, Late Bronze Age: two sphinxes alongside a naked goddess. The depiction of the sphinx with the Aegean wing and curly chest hair may be suggestive of Mycenaean influence (see Crowly 1989:39 n. 8 concerning Tamvaki 1974 and the "Aegean Prototype").

Plate 6:5 – lens (shaped) seal from Enkomi, Cyprus, Late Bronze Age. The goddess is seated with lions on both sides, surrounded by rosette decorations, wearing a scaled dress(?).

Plate 7:1 – a cylindrical seal from Cyprus, Late Bronze Age. A series which describes the repetitive goddess motif, the one standing close to the other with animals at her sides. The rosettes decoration also appears here.

The goddess mistress of the animals' motif is also known to us from Minoan and Mycenaean art, particularly on seals from the Late Bronze Age. The following are several examples (for details see in the list of plates):

Plate 7: 2, 3 – lens seals from Crete and Vaphio: the figure appears grasping only one animal, an interesting fact in itself, and of course esthetically and symbolically deviant from the generally accepted array.

Plate 7:4 on a lens seal from the Aegean Sea region, there is an interesting and fairly unique scene of the goddess holding a griffin rising up on its hind legs, much like a pet dog, facing the goddess. This interesting description creates the impression of absolute control over the animal or half-breed, which is usually threatening, and the emergence of a mutual affection occurring from this intimacy.[60]

Plate 7:5 – a Mycenaean lens seal, figure with two pouncing lions.

Plate 7:6 – see here also in illustration no. 7 – a lens seal from Vaphio. The goddess grasps the necks of two swans.

Plate 7:7 – (and illustration no. 7) a lens seal from Crete. Here too, the goddess is holding two swans with spread wings or in mid flight.

It is therefore an interesting comparison with the Potnia Theron or Artemis figure that appears in the Alabastron frieze from the EC period (see illustration no. 5). The figure with spread wings stands in its archaic format in the center of a decorative scheme popular during the period (including the background filled with rosettes in the famous Horror vacui style. By the way, the rosettes decoration was characteristic also of this early period of presenting the goddess and filling in the empty space, although not quite as densely. As said, see plate 7:1). It can definitely be seen in the detailed description of the figure (particularly compared to the figure in plate 7:7), positioning of the scene and the other decorative elements, as a motif taken from the original prototype found in these early examples.

Illustration no. 7
Two samples from plate 7:6, 7

Plate 7: 8 – a seal from Pylos. The figure is holding two dolphins.

In existing Mesopotamian tradition prototypes, the motif began as an expression of control over animals in the form of feeding (practically, feeding the animals) and later, submission by holding or standing calmly with the animals positioned next to the goddess. Subsequently, the dressed divine and human figures, with the animals alongside, had added details from the later Ianna-Ishtar iconographic lexicon of the Mari region: special attire, wings, weapons and various versions of the naked goddess.

In the Aegean region this motif appears during the Late Minoan and the Mycenaean period. The attire is Aegean,

---

[59] Assumption that this is a masculine type "Master of Animals" and a variation of the motif under discussion, see Crowly 1989:28, fig. 65.

[60] For other examples that represent the element of submission or of intimate relations with the goddess of any other patron, see Crowly 1989: Figs 73, 90, 124, 167, 170, 172. For example, in fig. 124 the griffin appears in a depiction on the back of a Mycenaean ring seal in the form of a pet or tamed animal and perhaps royal animal seated alongside its master the king. By the way, the griffin is perhaps the most

common oriental motif assimilated in Mycenaean art. For Minoan and Mycenaean griffin iconography and its progression from oriental tradition see Crowly 1989:52 n. 2, Tamvaki 1974, Frankfort 1936-7, Bisi 1965:22-106.

however many of the iconographic details are characteristic of the oriental world (other than the warlike element and the feeding issue which, as said, appears infrequently). The power of the goddess does not come as a challenge to the animals. In general they are relaxed and quiet. The accompanying animals, like in the East, are lions, bulls, sheep and mythical figures such as sphinxes and griffins. Lions are preferred.

New types are added in Mycenaean art, as well as from the Minoan heritage: birds, swans and dolphins.[61]

A.6 THE POTNIA THERON MOTIF ON ARYBALLOS VESSELS – THE ASSOCIATED OR ACCOMPANYING FIGURES AND MOTIFS

On the Aryballoi, this goddess motif is characteristic of principal theme scenes during the TR period and during the EC and MC periods, when it began to expire and disappear along with other themes characteristic of the Orientalizing period. The subject was expressed in the works of painters such as: the Potnia Painter, the Typhon Painter and the Royal Library Painter – during the EC period, and the Chimaera Painter during the MC period.

The figure generally appears irrespective of the surroundings, however there are figures that sometimes appear and may be identified with it: the Spinning Woman figure or the figures of the Padded Dancers, and no less interesting is the Women's Festival motif known as "Frauenfest" its German terminology. These motifs may occur within the context of local rituals for the goddess.[62]

Amyx mentions Payne's diagnosis concerning the painting combination on Corinthian vessels between the chain of dancing women together with the Padded Dancers motif (these appear particularly on two vessels, Amyx 1988 II:653), but does not research the subject nor ponder the significance of this combination. Jucker (1963, 47-61) examines the subject in depth in her research on the Frauenfest motif and the group of dancing women scene, and proposes adding the Padded Dancers motif as an additional aspect of a single ritual festival designed, eventually, to honor the goddess Artemis. The motif would generally appear to be independent and not necessarily have any narrative connection to the additional figures or to any additional activity that insinuates the nature of the ritual.

On the other hand, there are quite a few examples where the dancers are accompanied by certain props, sufficiently obvious, distinguishing ritual acts that pertain to this ritual - for example, holding together bouquets of flowers to form a chain of dancers. Two painters, mainly the Skating Painter and the Patra Painter specialize in these theme and motifs and combine these two motifs of male and female dancers (Seeberg 1971:222, Jucker 1963: Pl 22,Amyx 1988 Cat 229:185-189). The examples of the Skating Painter also include an additional line of figures shrouded in cloaks and forming a procession that belongs to the same ritual happening. The women obviously belong to the two other groups. There is an actual connection between the leading woman and the "Padded Dancer" facing her.[63]

There are reasons for connecting the Potnia Theron/Artemis ritual to this chain of figures, mainly because the ritual was very common particularly in Corinth.[64]

The prominent characteristics of the dancers or "Frauenfest" motif, protected and commanded by the goddess (Plate 8: 1-4) are the dancing women and the girls adorned with flowers, playing musical instruments, carrying trays of offerings, drinking and eating as well as weaving and spinning yarn. The "Padded Dancers" motif as well, with the somewhat wanton and soliciting nature in the presentation of their dance – all are in character with the rituals of the goddess of growth and fertility.[65]

Within context of this subject, there is an interesting finding of ritual nature from the 7th century BC, probably an oriental import (Phoenician or Syrian) found in Corinth: a clay plaque relief showing Astarte in a familiar fertility pose: with one hand on her breasts and the other on the pubic area (Boardman 1985:72-3, fig. 21a,b).[66]

A.7 THE PADDED DANCERS MOTIF (Plate 4:10)

The motif appears during the periods between the TR period until the LC-I period. During the EC period and beginning of the MC period the motif is widespread appearing on Corinthian vessels and particularly on the globular Aryballoi. The motif is performed by artists that specialize in the subject. Over time the subject spreads to

---

[61] For motif details characteristically associated with origin and sources, such as the attire, etc., see Barrelet 1955 and Tamvaki 1974 for comparisons with parallel motifs. In addition see Crowly 1989:34-39 for development and merging of oriental motifs in the Aegean tradition. Especially interesting is the example of combined iconography where the goddess is dressed in Minoan tradition. She is standing on Scale Mountain, the residence of the Mesopotamian gods (Crowly 1989:39, fig 349).

[62] For a direct connection (?) between the Spinning Woman and the goddess as well as between the Padded Dancers and the goddess, see examples on the Alabastra vessel, Amyx 1988:Pl 48:2a-b. For the Frauenfest motif see Calliopolitis-Feytmans 1970:47-65.

[63] The scenes are depicted on the Pyxide, Alabastra and other vessels, however there are examples that appear for example on a round Aryballos fragment by the Welcome Painter (Amyx 1988:Cat.102, A-8), although here the expression is slightly different, for example the sprinters connected to the woman even though she does not necessarily belong to the ritual.

[64] In general, Jucker 1963 and Harlow 1977 for the ritual details in general, and home practices concerning the Spinning Woman and the spindle in particular: Jucker 1963:57, n.69.

[65] The proximity and logical connection to Artemis rituals contradict Payne's traditional opinion (Payne 1931:121) who associates all of these to the Dionysian rituals. I think, therefore, that it is important to examine the persuasive references of Amyx (1988:656-7) although Payne's opinion, which also points to the possible integration of both rituals in their most ancient format, should not be dismissed. More about this in the discussion on the Padded Dancers motif.

[66] See also Burkert 1992:22, 96-100 relating to these works and their associated implications,

other artists, who add the motif to the other subjects they deal with.

As said, the motif appears mainly on the Aryballoi and Alabastra associated with drinking, such as various types of cups, Oinochoe and Kraters. Seeberg (1971) studied the subject and did not find any clear connection as to why it appears on the Aryballos and Alabastron more than on any other vessel.

General opinion is that these figures are not mythological, demonian or proto-satyrs, but rather "ordinary people expressing themselves in a certain way" to celebrate an event.[67]

The exaggerated physical padding characterizes the dancers and is easily discernable. In general the dance or conduct of the figures is usual, however sometimes the dancers are associated with drinking and lust. They too are generally shown without any attributes and are placed among regular or demonian animals or sirens, which flank them on both sides (by the Otterlo Painter, plate 8:5).

The painting of dancers, particularly on the Aryballoi, became sloppy over time, "going through the motions" as it were, or common, commercial expression, which also occurred with the progression of the warriors or four petals motifs.

It should be noted that the dancers also participate in parodies or in the Return of Hephaistos subject, in an emphasized act with his leg deformed, expressed also in the dancers. This segment does in fact belong to the Dionysian scene, and leading Payne to the assumption that they too are part of this scene.[68]

As has already been pointed out, the combination of the dancers motif with the group of female dancers in the Frauenfest, associated perhaps with the Artemis ritual, is pointing out some sort of association with that ritual. This may be an early development expressed in the integration of both rituals. In any event, as proposed by Jucker (1963:59), these rituals are Fertility Rites, that can be associated with the Potnia Theron ritual, an Oriental motif, the local Artemis or perhaps Dionysus.
During the LC-I period there are expressions of sexual scenes or a combination of the Padded Dancers with naked women, which appear on larger vessels, such as kraters. There is also an obvious beginning of Attic influence.[69]

A.8 THE POTNIA THERON MOTIF – PRESENTATION AND DISCUSSION OF ACCOMPANYING FINDINGS

In order to get a wider basis for discussion and conclusion, it is important to present the Potnia Theron motif, as it appears in a series of different findings from the period discussed in this work. The following are several examples:

Plate 9:1-2 – a bronze tray (Tondo) from the Idaean cave and mountain in Crete, around 700 BC. The frieze or upper band of the base has the goddess or lady mistress of the animals' motif.[70] The sphinxes are presented in a heraldic manner (under the central medallion). The goddess is naked and her hair style and the lions she is holding (by their ears (!) heads faced frontally) are completely oriental in design (Hampe-Simon 1981:167-168). The Tondo may have been imported from the East or made locally by eastern immigrants.

Plate 10:1-2 – The Potnia Theron motif appears on a large ceramic vessel: the Amphora of Boeotia, around 680 BC. The shape of the Amphora shows its Urartu origin. These vessels were most probably transferred through the Cyclades and Euboea to Boeotia.

The figure here is frontally depicted and the general scene with its accompanying components, like the former, is one of the earliest descriptions of this motif in 1st Millennium Greece. The previous descriptions, as said, are from the Minoan and Mycenaean period. The scheme, presented in the oriental version of heraldic fashion, is repeated and expressed again in the Aegean world during this period. The same applies to additional figures and motifs, such as the Griffins and Sphinxes. The goddess description is very schematic and clumsy, particularly the facial expression (this may be a copy of a relief as suggested by Hampe-Simon 1981:159). However, the motif is undoubtedly inspired by the Orient. The description of the fish ornamenting the front of her dress or her undergarment is interesting.

It is possible that the two zigzag lines descending from her hips symbolize the top of the mountain on which she is standing.[71] Strips of fabric are placed on her arms like wings. With this she protects and controls the animals. Two animal organs, the head and leg of the bull, "floating" in the background under her arms-wings, probably symbolize the ritual of offerings to the gods, rituals that were conducted by the priests of the goddess Artemis-Hekate, who appears here and seems to control, most probably, all of the animals in the frieze on the other side (see Plate 10:2): rabbits, birds of prey, ducks and even snakes in other friezes.

[67] Payne 1931:120, it should also be noted that the Proto-Corinthian Aryballos from Brindisi with a description of sexual aggression, where researcher Lo Porto attributes the figure to the "proto-satyr and Dionysos Amyx 1988:659.98, but there is no evidence of Dionysian ritual at this early stage of Corinthian art!
[68] Repeated in another example where a leopard skin is worn by one of the figures in the scene on the Aryballos (Payne 1931:515, Seeberg 1971:no.218). Amyx gives an additional example of a man carrying grapes on his shoulder (Amyx 1988:Cat.110, no.C-8).
[69] And in the better known performance of the common Satyrs and Menades scene. See Amyx 1988 II:n. 97 on the Neck Amphora.

[70] The essential connection between the subject of this work and the artistic expression in the framework of oriental metal plates, and on the Cretan center and the Daedalic style will be discussed later, on pages 21-26 and in Appendix 3, pp. 46-47.
[71] See a precedent of this from the Minoan period at Hampe-Simon 1981:fig.441 which brings us back to the element of positioning divine figures on the top of Scale Mountain, residence of the Mesopotamian gods.

Plate 10:3 – a terracotta bowl from Rhodes, around 630 BC. The Gorgon that appears here is the figure of Potnia Theron, an interesting combination in itself. The Gorgon has eyes open wide and a split tongue. She has a diadem or crown on her forehead; her hair falls to the side of her head and in front like a beard. Four wings separate the head from the body (a fault in the painting expression, I do not think there is any symbolic insinuation here). She has a belt on her waist. A muscular leg protrudes from her gown that has slits to illustrate the folds. The complex figure is in the familiar Potnia Theron pose holding in her hands the necks of two water birds (tamed swans?), one on each side. The front leg, the arms and bird wings, are all decorated with filling decorations. The wings scheme is expressed in Archaic-oriental style. The elegant protrusion of the feet from the concentric circle should be noted, as a sign of over-sophistication and the creation of dimensions, as well as a breakthrough (also literally) in an attempt to escape the previous rigid frameworks.

This may also be a human figure wearing the Gorgon mask and therefore, the entire scene – with the placing of the birds on the winged dress and the knee, as well as the protrusion of the muscular leg from the fold of the dress and the feet from the frame – takes on a theatrical, humorous nature. In any event there is significant decorative and stylish progression here or perhaps a new ideological concept.

The fact that the vessel comes from Rhodes serves to reinforce the role of the place as an important and influential creative center that promoted, as a transitional place, the oriental elements on to Greece and the islands.[72]

Plate 11:3 – A plate covering a golden brooch from Rhodes, around 630 BC, another of the earliest examples of the Potnia Theron motif in an impressive frontal presentation. The metal work and miniature decoration are remarkable. The figure holds the tails of two lions in her hands. The two lions have their heads turned looking upwards at the goddess, in a roar of submission. The goddess is winged, her head and hair are styled like the

lion's mane similar to a design describing the sphinxes. Her facial expression is similar to the style characteristic of the Korai maidens (the Korai sculptures, during their early stages but slightly later than this period) with the famous "archaic smile" that appears at the beginning of the period (see Richter 1974: figs. 58, 66-95, or Boardman 1996: figs. 71, 108).

If we return and compare to the painting on the Corinthian Alabastron (Illustration no. 5, EC period) a work made in Corinth during the same period, and compare presentation of the figure expressed mainly with the uplifted wings and lifted long dress, although with a slightly different pattern (diamond as compared to square) – we shall see that the use of the motif in this oriental style was significant and contemporary in these different and important places.[73]

Plate 13:3 – An ivory plate from a brooch worn in the temple of Artemis Orthia in Sparta, from the mid 7th century BC. The figure of the goddess Artemis or in its present format of the winged Potnia Theron, wears a crown of leaves and holds the necks of large birds (perhaps crows) that have their heads lifted towards her in submission. The decorative work is rough and somewhat clumsy with geometric-schematic expression, but there is no doubt that the mastery of the goddess over the animals is tangible and emphasized. The detailed presentation of the figure (such as the raised wings and the dress design) and the scene array is characteristic of the motif and reminiscent of the expressions on the items previously discussed and in the earlier Oriental and Aegean examples (Crowly 1989:34-39).[74]

This description of the goddess wearing the crown or Polus is associated with another item from the temple of Artemis Orthia in Sparta, Plate 13:4 – a bust of the goddess from the end of the 7th century BC, rather elegantly made of bone. The goddess wears a polus decorated with leaves or floral tongues. The frontal emphasis is impressive, despite the proportional inaccuracy in description of the parts such as the nose, lips and ears, and particularly the hairstyle and long neck (like a long stylized mane) bestowing an animal cat or sphinx-like appearance. The fact of this being the specific goddess belonging to the Potnia Theron motif and the

---

[72] Of what is happenings on the islands such as Rhodes, Crete, Samos, Delos, Aegina and Euboea during the PC and Corinthian periods and the attribution of various findings, other than the Cypro-Phoenician ceramic to the Phoenician and oriental material can be seen at Markoe 1985:125. He relates to studies by Coldstream and Boardman that have been mentioned in this work. For the appearance of oriental motifs, such as the appearance of the Cypro-Phoenician bull or the static or attacking warrior, the lines of animals and the offering processions of the dancing women holding hands such as the Frauenfest motif, together with the Greek repertoire such as the Homeric scenes, the chariot processions and the description of mythological animals such as the Chimera, Pegasus and Centaurs – see Kraiker 1951:Pl. 27:342, the works of the painter known as the Round Dance painter, at Demargne 1964 fig. 439, Boardman 1975a:fig. 36 and Cook 1997:41ff.Pls. 9-10. For Phoenician and Cypro-Phoenician material from Rhodes and the Dodecanese in general and for influences earlier than the 9th century BC from Cyprus and mainly from Kythion – see Karageorghis 1976:95ff. Also see the research by Negbi concerning the presence and earlier influences of the Phoenicians at Mediterranean sites including Rhodes and the Dodecanese, which were reached (Rhodes) by the Cypro-Phoenician material already in the second half of the 11th century BC, Negbi 1992:606-607.

[73] A very similar oriental format of the figure and the sophisticated miniature work and perhaps even of the motif, although difficult to prove, characterizes the five gold platelets from Rhodes (Plate 12:2) from the second half of the 7th century BC, which in delicate and beautiful relief work, depict a goddess, probably of the bees (Melissai), although she can very reasonably be identified as Artemis or as the Anatolian Kybele, (see Hampe-Simon 1981:212). The goddess is winged with the body of a bee, her arms are slightly lifted and fisted as if grasping something in her hands; her head, face and hairstyle appear, as previously, like the Kore in Plate 12:3 in oriental style and in the earlier format.

[74] And in examples just as tangible resultant of an earlier development of the figures and an emphasis mainly on describing the face in profile such as the example at Hampe-Simon 1981: fig. 435, an individual description of the goddess figure (her head in profile and the rest of her body frontal) and especially in the clothing, which appears on a piece of relief from a large Pithos from the Cyclades from the second quarter of the 7th century BC.

expressive fashion in the animal-like (albeit delicate) description of the goddess, leads to a somewhat earlier context of women or goddesses from the East wearing a polus, given adequate expression in the ivory works.[75]

In creating the motif framework associated with the goddess rituals, motifs discussed earlier, such as the Frauenfest or the Padded Dancers, the leading painter specializing in this last motif, known as The Welcome Painter, illustrated the air of celebration and added demonic creatures to the jolly figures. The siren wearing the polus or crown (with the characteristic spread wings) fits into the fine composition created by the artist on the globular Aryballos from the EC period (end of the 7th century BC, Illustration no. 8).

Illustration no. 8
Globular Aryballos from the EC period
(625-590 BC, Amyx 1988:Pl. 45:1a-b)

In creating this array of components that characterize the main scene, it is interesting to see the painter's combination of elements and figures accompanying this specific ritual. The characteristic siren wearing the polus or crown appears here in the oriental format characteristic of the griffin and sphinx presented in this manner in many other examples.[76]

Within this context it is important to take time over another representative example that guides us to the coming subjects associated to influences on metal work and ceramic vessels work in general and the Aryballoi in particular: a crowned sphinx in a similar display that appears as a central figure and component, in a comprehensive example that combines the elements comprising the decorative framework in its oriental format. This somewhat early expression, from the mid 7th century BC appears on a Dinos from Arkades with three plastic busts (Protomoi) of griffins (Plate 29: 1,2). The vessel replaced the accepted bronze vessel with the griffin's bust and served as an urn in the Arkades necropolis, south-east Crete (for details see following pages 27-28).

The use of ceramic vessels, which, as said, took over from the oriental metal vessel as the object for painting

and sculpture, provides a new and original dimension, even more so than the work done on the metal vessels.

A.8.1 PRESENTATION AND DISCUSSION OF ASSOCIATED FINDING - THE DECORATIVE STYLE, THE MODELS AND MOTIFS

THE ARYBALLOS AND THE PHOENICIAN METAL BOWLS

The Greek potters of Corinth, particularly those that painted the decorations on the ceramics (a subject that was rather neglected by the Oriental potters) welcomed the variety of new models and motifs that came in from the east. It can once again be said, that the Greeks were waiting for a more realistic artistic style: one that would integrate with their geometric art, especially on the figurative plane, that would receive the delicacy, the precision in details and the required flexibility in describing narrative scenes designed to illustrate the reality and fantasy they had been wanting to express for a long time.[77]

All the decorative components expressed in the paintings on the Aryballoi – in terms of the floral decorations that appeared mainly and over time in the top frieze, such as the palmette among the rosette stars and water birds, and the figurative items in the central frieze, that will be described in the following – originated from the prototypes on the Phoenician plates (Paterae).

During the styles development process, the decorative style known as the Black Figure Style, during the PC period, and the characteristic use of incision to emphasize outlines, announce the introduction of a completely new repertoire of subjects and motifs in Greece. A substantial portion emanate directly from the iconographic lexicon of the Phoenician works, especially in terms of decorative technique and ideology, from the metal plates.

As said, a style element significantly dominant in the varied vessels is the use of incision to emphasize body parts of the various figures. From then on the use of incision was used in the Black Figure Style, to emphasize outlines as well. This style did not exist in ceramics but was common in metal works. The models used by the local potters were the Phoenician metal plates (see examples at Demargne 1964:333ff, figs. 434-438, 440 and at Boardman 1985: fig. 53). One of the typical vessels used by the artists to transmit the acquired style and technique was the Aryballos. Besides the technical use of incision, the vessel was used generally because of its size, with emphasized refinement, as a prominent milestone in the process of borrowing oriental motifs,

[75] See for example Barnett 1982: Pls. 43-44, from the 9th century BC. However, the motif in this form, reached even later stages and the 6th century BC, see the stone head of the goddess Hera from Olympia, around 580 BC, at Boardman 1996: fig. 73.
[76] See for example the golden sphinx from Perachora near Corinth from the last quarter of the 7th century BC, Plate 4:4, or Hampe-Simon 1981: fig. 411. This motif on the present Aryballos, see also Seeberg 1971:35.

[77] It should once again be remembered, as previously written, that during the Geometric period, which began during the 9th century BC, oriental influences were already discerned. See for example: Coldstream 1977: Chap.15 on the breaking down of rigidity and the transition to the realistic delicacy of the Orient, which was also the determining flow everywhere. See also the Proto-Corinthian Aryballos from 700 BC which shows the beginnings of engraving attempts, Coldstream 1977:173, n.14, fig. 56b-c.

particularly those that appear in the Cypro-Phoenician tradition: for example the tuft or curl on the birds heads or the mythical creatures such as the Griffin, which is identical to the same motif in the earlier Cypro-Phoenician tradition and even from the Minoan and Mycenaean period (see Frankfort 1936-1937, Bisi 1956:22-106, Tamvaki 1974 and Crowly 1989:52 and for example Plate 15:4, 6). To these can be added the appearance of other elements, such as the technical description of the wing emerging from the shoulder and not the back, exactly like those that appear on the Phoenician plates (Markoe 1985:122, n.168).

At a later stage, during the PC period, the borrowing of Cypro-Phoenician motifs was found also with known painters, such as the Corneto Painter, the Toulouse Painter, the Ajax Painter and the Aetos Painter. It is evident in the description of the bull, for example, in the Cypro-Phoenician style: with the tail curling down, that appears on vessels made by the Aetos Painter, or another motif of the lion and hero's struggle scene, where the lion is characterized by placing its forelegs on the hero's arm, a description found for instance of an Aryballos vessel from the MPC period, made by the painter known as Ajax (Markoe 1985:122nts. 169-170).[78]

During the late PC period and throughout the Corinthian period, as said, there is an actual absorption of oriental motifs that characterize metal vessels, such as the Cypro-Phoenician bull, figures of warriors, and as said, lines of animals and festive processions of dancing women (see note 79). At the same time a local repertoire of Homeric and accompanying scenes such as chariot processions and descriptions of mythological animals, such as the chimers, Pegasus and centaurs, began to develop.

Additional decorative motifs, figures such as a soldier, rider and scenes such as a dog chasing a deer, which turns its head and a hawk flying above, are some of the characteristic items transferred from the metal vessels (Illustration no. 10). It is no coincidence that these figures, for example, are principle figures found on the Phoenician plates and bowls in a variety of Etrurian vessels.[79]

Illustration no. 10
Central frieze on Proto-Corinthian Aryballos
(by the painter known as Evelyn, p.25) according to Plate 1: 7,8. At Neeft 1988: fig.15a

An additional and interesting aspect as already mentioned appears on this last Aryballos: the combination of figures

is significant because here for the first time is an example of a frieze with a narrative description within framework of the Proto-Corinthian repertoire.[80] This division into two, the soldier and rider on the one side of the combination and the deer hunt on the other side, appears on Phoenician plates. In addition, a pair of curling palmettes that emphasizes the central frieze in one format or another, also appears many times in the decorations of Phoenician plates.

A.9 THE "TREE OF LIFE" MOTIF

A common motif (as seen on the right side of the frieze and in the center of the rolling combination in illustration no. 10 – of the Proto-Corinthian Aryballos) like the Tree of Life common in the orient[81] and in the incision art of the metal vessels, which unites the heraldic array of groups of animals or mythical beasts such as Sphinxes and Griffins on both sides or two scenes connected to one subject without any clear narrative – appears here as a motif or functional plant combination for similar purposes.

Interesting in itself as a comparison (Plate 16:1) is the expression (perhaps the pioneer or prototype of the Attic motif) of the motif on a Proto-Attic jar (early Oinochoe, according to the trifoliate rim), from around 700 BC, where two stylized versions of the oriental Tree of Life appear as a decorative and isolated combination without the characteristic format alongside. On the lower of the two to the left side there are rosette flowers with black and white petals with a long, rounded flowering stem at the end. On the right side, coiled branches emerge from the trunk with buds at their ends. The motif is repeated in early Mesopotamian and Aegean iconography,[82] designed, as said, to serve as an object centralizing groups of animals on both sides that are associated with ceremonial scenes and/or of course as a decorative object designed to focus the eye to the center. Examples of the motif in its early format are in Plate 17:1 – a seal from the Uruk period and on a segment of stone slab (Stela) in Plate 17:2 – from the Neo-Sumerian period. Also samples from Mari, in Plate 17:3 – segment of a fresco, and a seal and ring from Mycenae in Plate 17:4, 5.

An interesting combination of the Tree of Life motif on an Aryballos (illustration no. 11) that appears at a

---

[78] On the Aryballos from the MPC period, the researcher provides a reference to earlier and later Aryballoi, in the transfer of these oriental and Cypro-Phoenician motifs from metal vessel works (such as the palmette with the double voluta) to Aryballoi and other Corinthian vessels, Markoe 1985:121-123.

[79] As said, on demand of the local population. See Markoe 1985:191 ff and no. E2,3,6 or at Moscati 1988:445.

[80] On all matters pertaining to the figures and the narrative aspect on Proto-Corinthian vessels, see the interesting study by Benson1995:163-177, Pl. 37, who brings examples from Ashmolean and Samos, see ibid fig. 1. In reference to his previous article: Benson 1995:163-164 concerning an earlier period that concerns our matter as well: Benson 1995a:335-361, the researcher attributes the figures and scenes to sophistication derived from the attitude to the myth, the symbolism and the Homeric epos. On the other hand, there is no connection to the source or inspiration, as a rule, in the issue of artistic influence on the technique and style achieved by this or another artist in describing those scenes but rather a hint of something local that developed and improved (Benson 1995:170).

[81] See for example within framework of the ivory works from Nimrud, at Barnett 1957:138 and in subjects of the Layard group at Crowly 1989:64ff as said, on the motif from the orient and its early sources.

[82] At Crowly 1989:64-69 – who emphasizes the Early Bronze Age and development of a secondary motif in Aegean art: the Sacred Pillar.

relatively early stage, i.e., at the transition stage between the EPC and the MPC periods[83], sharpens and emphasizes the motif and other items with strong outlines, which fill the entire space of the central frieze on the globular Aryballos (which appears without the rim and handle, questioning the originality associated with this fact - see references in the note). The lower frieze emphasizes the rays motif emanating from the flat base.

Illustration no. 11
The Tree of Life motif on an EPC Aryballos
(EPC-MPC I according to Amyx 1988:Pl. 2)

Use of an additional motif, the rays motif mentioned mainly in the format of pointed rays emanating from the base upwards, was common in oriental metal vessels and in other art works (by nature, as assumed earlier, it was also a plant motif resembling thorn like flowering or the lotus, and see plates 18, 19, 1, 3).[84]

A nice example, Plate 16:2 and illustration no. 11a, of a Proto-Corinthian Aryballos from around 630 BC, which emphasizes the characteristic rays or thorns format emanating from the vessel base and the acquired engraving tradition: in the central frieze the sphinxes are seated in heraldic format (with a duck in between), the wings are gathered together and raised in upward rounded oriental style. The description of the bodies is more anatomically detailed and the outlines were made with delicate incision, particularly the description of the woman's head (?), the hair and mane.

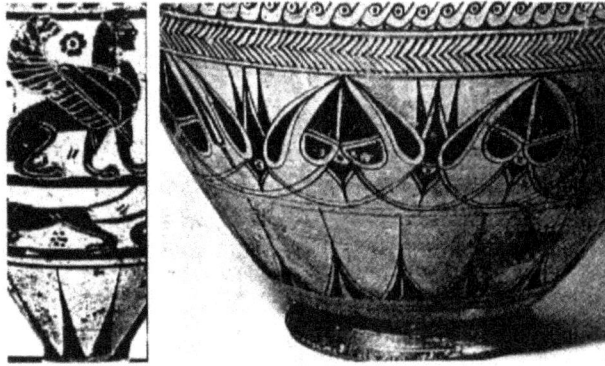

Illustration no. 11a
The characteristic rays motif that appears on the base of the Proto-Corinthian Aryballos (to the left, around 630 BC, detail from Plate 16:2), and at the base of an Oinochoe from the beginning of the 6th century BC (indicating the origins and see note 84 below).

A.10 METAL PLATES AND BOWLS

In order to better understand the scale of the oriental schools' influence on style and technique and the complexity of transferring the oriental motifs to Greece, it is important to retrieve and present examples from research literature of well known groups of vessels from Olympia, Perachora, Kerameikos in Athens (where together with Proto-Attic and Proto-Corinthian ceramic vessel, bronze bowl, known as the Frauenprotome Bronze Bowls were found, dated at 700 BC)[85] and vessels from Crete (Idaean cave) – and to take time for an analysis of the finding and a comparative discussion.[86]

In designing and decorating metal vessels such as the Phoenician bronze and silver plates, prominent motifs and items appear that are important to mention, because they are passed on to the local decorative framework of Greece and to local ceramic vessels in a process of imitation and assimilation: and for example, a continuous frieze of animals such as the bulls moving in a sort of procession.[87] The influence is obvious not only in the subject matter in general but also in the individual design of the components. Even in the description of motifs and other scenes such as the tribute processions in honor of various deities the Phoenician model is present.[88]

A finding from the Attic group (Plate 20:1): a Proto-Attic clay plate found at Karameikos illustrates the extent to

---

[83] At Amyx 1988:Pl.2, 3a-b, around the end of the 8th century, quoting Payne. The latter assumes this is an expression of the beginning of the Black Figures style. As expressed here, use of engraving for emphasis acquired from the metal works is minimal in any event.

[84] See for example Markoe 1985:316, G3 in the metal plates, or from a series of plant motifs in the catalog of ivory works from Nimrud, at Barnett 1957:Pl.LXXXI, Pl. XC, s317, s322, see Plate 19:1-2: a series of lotus petals from ivory (used as handles for accessories) from the 9th century BC from Nimrud and also Plate19:3: a Phoenician ivory panel showing a young man holding a lotus, from Nimrud, 9th century BC, or a Phoenician ivory platelet, also from Nimrud, from the 8th century BC, describing Horus the child seated on a lotus flower, Moscati 1988:413.

The Greek ceramic examples are countless: see for example Arias-M. Hirmer 1962:Pls. VI, VII, X, and at this opportunity the comparison made by Arias and Hirner with vessels with the same motif from Chios (fig. 28) showing the distribution in the Asia Minor region and particularly and Oinochoe from Rhodes (fig. 26) showing the origin of the motif: the lotus and buds in the bottom frieze. See with double emphasis at Boardman 1975a:fig. 43: the rays motif on the bottom frieze and above it the lotus, definitely a convincing continuity. See also Plate 18: Wild Goat Style Oinochoe[83] from the beginning of the 6th century BC.

[85] At Kübler 1939-80, Vol.VI:120ff, Markoe 1985:121, n.163 – firstly and mainly Kübler followed by Markoe, give special mention of the direct connection with the east by examining these vessels that arrived from north Syria.

[86] Studies on the subject, beginning with Lamb 1929 and Kunze 1931 and later ones by Borell 1978 and of course Kübler 1939-80, and the comprehensive and exhaustive material and discussion of oriental influences at Markoe 1985.

[87] This frieze has direct attribution to a group of motifs that appear in Phoenician art. Prototypes of this motif appear on plates found in Greece. See Markoe 1985:119, n. 150 and particularly examples G5, G6, G9, G10.

[88] For example a miniature gift vessel a shield made of terracotta found in the temple of Hera at Tiryns and belonging to the Late Geometric period (dating: end of 8th century BC/beginning of 7th century BC, by definition fits a transition period), describes a scene amazingly compatible with the Phoenician prototype, itself processed by the Phoenicians from the Egyptian origin. See Markoe 1985:119.

which the Phoenician metal plate model was copied freely: the subject, the style and the iconographic elements. The style (according to components of the Aryballos artistic analysis) ranges between the late Geometric period and the Archaic period. Some elements from the late Geometric period have remained. The plate is dated at 670 BC.[89]

The plate is flat with omega shaped handles, clearly imitating the metal prototype of Phoenician plates. The subject: a medallion of rosettes surrounded by two rounded strips, each containing a description of animals in a procession and in different positions separate from each other in a rounded stripe of the geometric motif (graduated-oblique) – compatible with the Phoenician model. The use of incision to mark the outlines and internal details in the description of the animals, etc., as expressed in this example, was also common in the decorative designs works on metal vessels. In addition, on all matters pertaining to presentation of the subject and to the proportions in positioning the images and all the components of the general depiction: the bulls depicted in profile (one horn and one ear, head down), the neck line, the lion's mane, the drooping tail, features mainly on the two bulls in the outer strip – are compatible with the Cypro-Phoenician source.[90]

There is also an appearance, at least three times, of a common Syrian Phoenician motif: the cow suckling the calf. This motif appears often in ivory and bronze Phoenician works.[91]

Another well known motif, yet original in its current form, appears here without precedent in the image of the spotted deer (on the inner strip). The male partner, incidentally in this original version, also appears for the first time on a slightly earlier Proto-Corinthian Aryballos.[92] However, as said, even the prototype of the spotted deer in similar versions, appears regularly on Cypro-Phoenician bowls from Cyprus and Etruria.[93]

The spotted animal decoration in this style also appears in other scenes. Description of the spotted sphinx in the Proto-Corinthian format characteristic of the middle

period: the division into friezes (with figurative scenes, geometric combinations and floral formats), and the heraldic array of the central frieze that includes sphinxes in a characteristic position, can be found on a Proto-Corinthian Aryballos from around 675 BC (Illustration no. 12).

Illustration no. 12
Proto-Corinthian Aryballos, c. 675 BC
(Cook 1972, Pl. 9d)

It is interesting to find the repetitive animal (dogs) frieze as a continuation of an earlier tradition (taken from the early geometric framework, perhaps even sub-Mycenaean- Proto-Geometric, and see piriform Aryballos in illustration no. 2), however it "descended" from the shoulder to the center and later to the bottom part, as it appears here.

All the components mentioned, in the style and design and in the appearance of common motifs, indicate the obvious copying of the decorative format and style from Phoenician metal vessels. Other than the Proto-Attic plate mentioned here, the metal counterpart should be mentioned, which is found in a broken vessel that was found in a grave at Kerameikos together with two little bowls made of bronze from north Syria. In the frieze decoration there is an incised description of winged animals in the "orientalizing"[94] style and even surrounding the rosettes motif. Kübler (1939-1980) dates it at 700 BC, some 30 years prior to the date related to the Proto-Attic plate.

Incidentally, it should again be mentioned, that Proto-Corinthian vessels were found in graves at Kerameikos dated at this period (Proto-Attic) which demonstrates, among others (other than the more massive production of the Corinthian material) the integration of styles at the beginning of the period of dominant absorption of oriental motifs. Kübler's research already stated this as did Markoe (1985) who especially states the direct connection with the orient in vessels from north Syria (as said the bronze bowls known as Frauenprotome Bronze Bowls found in the graves at this site and that are dated at 700 BC, see p. 23).

---

[89] At Markoe 1985:121 (according to Kunze 1931 and Kübler 1959, 1970) dating illustrates the integration of periodical styles and the transporting of geometric decorative components to the late period, a subject we dealt with earlier.

[90] At Markoe 1985:120 who finds parallels at Borell 1978:55ff on all matters pertaining to comparisons with local Attic ceramics and particularly to Proto-Attic plates with oriental design ("an orientalizing Proto-Attic dish" is the terminology used by Markoe and Kubler).

[91] See for example ivory works from Nimrud from the north western palace at Barnett 1957:Pl.V, c23, 34, c22, 32, c29,31, 33 and on the source and progression of the motif Barnett 1957:143-5.

[92] See Cook 1972:3-4, 110-117, Pl.38-9 who examines aspects of this Aryballos with later samples of vessels from the LC period.

[93] According to the Phoenician models and see mainly Markoe 1985: Cy 6, E2, E6. See within this context the motif on ivories and copying of the oriental deer model (drinking or feeding in the meadow) in Greek art at Barnett 1957:152-153, who also mentions the motif that appears on the metal plate from Crete and that was transferred in this format to Greek art at the end of the 8th century BC – beginning of the 7th century BC.

[94] According to Kübler 1959, 1970:Vol. VI: 2, 227, 400, 557, fig. 69, Pls.22-23 – concerning this finding and the reference to the Proto-Attic plate mentioned above.

A.10.1. THE METAL PLATES AND BOWLS: DECORATION AND FUNCTION

The Phoenician bowls found in Greece are made of bronze, unlike those made of silver that were designed for use by the wealthy aristocratic classes, found in Etruria. The bowls presented on Plate 20:2, 3, found in Greece and Crete, were designed to serve local plebeian patrons and not aristocrats.

A large number of bowls was found in religious compounds and temples such as Delphi, Olympia, Rheneia, Perachora, the Acropolis in Athens and in the Idaean Cave in Crete. These findings illustrate the use made of the vessels for religious ritual rather than for burial purposes. In terms of functionality use of vessels resembles that of the Greek Phiale for ritual purposes, a vessel generally offered in tribute.[95] In other words, the Phoenician vessels were used and suited for the same purpose.

The scenes described on these vessels are also adapted to the buyer's position. There is symbolism such as the bull and lion illustration[96] or characteristic religious scenes such as offering processions, differing from the more common descriptions on the Etrurian plates designated for aristocratic addresses, and which deal mainly with military processions or hunting scenes. On the other hand, there are vessels in Greece (such as the vessels on Plate 21:1-2, Plate 23:1,2) with more unusual scenes of hunting and war, characteristic of Greece, albeit with emphasis on mythology, as the chariot is harnessed to a sphinx (see Plate 21:1-2 and Plate 23:1).

The bowl on Plate 22:1 in style and shape (probably from Sparta, Markoe 1985:207), decorated with two strips, the inner with a row of bulls and the outer with an offering procession, is closer to the Cypro-Phoenician vessels in both style and iconographic expression.

The sphinx pulling the chariot and the archer at the back that appears on the plates in Plate 21:1-2 and Plate 23:2 from Olympia, were probably made by the same workshop. The row of lions in the inner strip of the bowl at the Ashmolean Museum (from Olympia, as said on Plate 23:2) constitutes an interesting version of the row of bulls from the characteristic frieze. The elongated torso of the lion, by the way, fits those of the bulls from the Fortetsa bowl, Crete on Plate 20:3.

As mentioned above, the bowls on Plate 21:1-2, and Plate 23:1,2 have similar iconographic elements that closely resemble several plates from Nimrud. The position of the charging lion with its head turned on the bowl on Plate

23:2 from the Ashmolean Museum, appears almost identically on a plate from Nimrud Plate 22:2. The lion scene on this bowl, on Plate 23:2, appears similarly on another plate from Nimrud (Markoe 1985, Comp.5). The internal division of the medallion on the Delphi bowl, Plate 21:1-2 and Plate 23:1, into three strips, appears on several plates from Nimrud.[97]

Bowls from Athens (see Markoe 1985:G2) and from Olympia (Plate 24:1-2 and Plate 25:1) have characteristic Egyptian style. The bowl from Olympia has a strip divided into four friezes with niches in between flanked with two papyrus pillars in the center of which are four divine images with a winged solar disc above their heads. The composition on one of the friezes, depicting the hero killing a griffin, closely resembles the Cypro-Phoenician plates (such as on Plates 25:2 and 26:1,2 from Idalion and Kurion) and motifs that appear on ivories from Nimrud (see Markoe 1985:124, n.175 such as the complex inner medallion, in Plate 24:1-2 and Plate 25:1). The same bowl mentioned above, from Athens, divided into four subjects that describe pairs of sphinxes close to the Holy Tree, by this design fits the division characteristic of the Egyptian style, i.e. the division into four repetitive motifs. Additional plates and bowls from Olympia and Rheneia, depict the bulls frieze known for its eclectic style.[98]

On all matters pertaining to dating of vessels and its significance: all the above examples, whether belonging by style and design to the homeland Phoenician workshop or from transitional centers of settlements in Greece, are dated at the second half of the 8th century BC. The bowl on Plate 27:1-2 from Kerameikos in Athens probably belongs to an earlier period of bowl making and is independent in this series of bowls from Greece. Unlike other examples mentioned from Greece (except perhaps on Plate 22:1) that have close parallels in Phoenician vessels probably manufactured in Phoenicia, the bowl from Kerameikos is identified with a Cyprian source of manufacture (probably, see Markoe 1985:124, 171, CY3) – to which another bowl from Idalion in Crete is compared in terms of style and decoration.

Unlike the vessels found in Greece, from the end of the Geometric period, i.e. the period between 750-700 BC, most of which present varying degrees of Egyptian influence (or Phoenician eclecticism, it should be noted), Plate 27:1-2 presents an earlier bowl from Kerameikos the iconography of which displays a Syrian-Hittite tradition of the beginning of the first millennium BC. Firstly, this is expressed in the faces of the figures, the Semite visual: the nose and almond shape eyes and the hairstyle on the female figures. The same applies to the animal descriptions: the mane and size of the lion's head and the prominent folds and lines in the bull's neck.[99]

---

[95] Like the bowl found in the Hera Limenaia temple in Perachora. See Markoe 1985:123. See also the Proto-Attic plate from Kerameikos (Plate 20:1) dated 670 BC, which illustrates the extent to which the Phoenician metal plate model was copied freehandedly: the subject, style and iconographic elements, Markoe 1985:121 (based on Kubler 1959,1970:VI and Kunze 1931).

[96] There are estimations concerning astrology, see Hopkins 1965:28ff and Markoe 1985:123, n.172.

[97] See Markoe 1985:124 according to Layard Pl. 59 A,D.

[98] Two from Olympia (see Markoe 1985:G5,6) and two from Rheneia, to which are added parts of vessels from an unknown source (Markoe 1985:U1-5) and fragments from a copper bowl from Nimrud (Markoe 1985:124, n. 176).

[99] Markoe's detailed and precise diagnosis concerning the iconographic origin belonging to such an early period, is especially interesting

This traditionally ancient depiction brings us back to other examples dealt within the artistic analysis framework belonging to the Aryballoi. There is no doubt that not only in terms of motif transition it is vital for understanding the centers of influence but also, where possible, the little components in individual description such as this latter one. A work designed to examine the chronological order in the process of motif introduction is not at all easy, and therefore, often the combination of descriptions, such as this latter one (within framework of the general subject of metal plates and bowls) is extremely significant and important for reinforcing the work's general hypothesis.

Let us return to this chapter's point of origin and re-emphasize the importance of the components that characterize the metal plates and bowls within framework of the Aryballoi artistic analysis discussion.

Boardman (1975a:41) writes that the Corinthian painters invented a new technique where the figures are painted by outlines (silhouettes style) but the details were expressed by incising in order to show the lighter shade of ceramic under the layer of color in more delicate lines. We have already learned that the incision method was accepted and common in the Orient, in metal works, such as the Phoenician plates or other oriental metal vessels with sculptured handled, and was also designed to delicately emphasize various anatomical and other details. Except for the effect of the incision in the ceramic painting, the method and idea already existed and in light of the available abundance of new elements, it was only natural for the Greek artist to use it as a means for developing artistic works using this new technique.

A.11. THE ARTISTIC STYLE IN OTHER VESSELS AND AREAS – COMPARATIVE PARALLELS

In order to position the subject within a more extensive general background, and connect it to a parallel process in the Greek art world, in adjacent and remote concentric geographic circles surrounding the research center – it is important to cover several examples (in the field of spatial research) that can contribute to and enrich us with additional, comparative material, in order to comprehend and enlighten the specific subject of this work.

An Attic drinking cup from the end of the Late Geometric period (720-700 BC on Plate 2:28) has a curious motif mentioned in association with the metal works and the subjects transferred to ceramic vessels, particularly to the Aryballoi: the inner frieze portrays bulls in a concentric procession of several circles, a subject as said, inspired by the Orient and in particular by metal works of Phoenician origin.[100]

These cups were found at burial sites such as the Athenian Kerameikos and others (see Hampe-Simon 1981: fig. 241). The three processional bulls, their bodies filled in with dark color, their heads schematically outlined. In this processional scene, the geometric characteristics began to breakdown: the lines are softened by waviness, and the characteristic zigzag is replaced with a curved line. In Corinth, at a parallel and identical stage of transition (around 700 BC), a very convincing description appears on the base of a Lekythos-Oinochoe (illustration no. 13) in a frieze that represents the peak of this process with all its components.

Illustration no. 13
Base of a Proto-Corinthian Lekythos-Oinochoe from around 700 BC
(according to Hampe-Simon 1981:248)

Attention should be given to the Dinos description that appears here prominently and centrally in oriental format.[101] Other geometric patterns and components appear here, as on the previous Attic cup, alongside new elements somewhat softened compared to the generally rigid geometric scenes. Especially obvious is the thick wavy line that meanders between the characteristic zigzag lines. The description of the animal and bird images in the new style is reminiscent of the Attic style differentiated by the rich details and sophistication that characterize the Corinthian one, expressed by the Evelyn painter in the early Proto-Corinthian Aryballos (at its later stage and alongside geometric plant filled examples, plate 1:7, 8 and the roll in illustration no. 10[102]).

In Athens there is a parallel process that unifies, among others, the components of continued early period traditions (Mycenaean): painting on the base of the Proto-

---

because of the significant tracking of a tradition began in the ancient oriental world, reached the archaic period and takes a dominant part and even reached the boundaries of the classical period, penetrating them. See Markoe 1985:124.

[100] In the oriental models there are inner friezes and the ceramic cups imitate these decorations in position (inner) but more modest. See extensively on the subject and on the Phoenician metal plates at Borell

1978 and particularly Markoe 1985 the chapter dealing with Phoencian influences. Especially interesting is the appearance of a motif in Greece at an earlier stage: a comparison can be made between the description of these bulls to those that appear on ceramic Kraters from the late Mycenaean period at Hanky 1967:107-148, Pls.26-37.

[101] And most probably in its metal format, see Coldstream 1977:358-366 where the researcher deals with the components of this subject in a chapter on the characteristics of oriental influences (Chap. 15: Oriental Influences).

[102] For the abundance of motifs and models that appear on this Aryballos and its uniqueness see also Amyx 1988:365-6.

Attic Dinos (Dinos-Cauldron, Plate 28:3) from around 700 BC, shows the rich and beautiful expression that appears on a large area that differs from the characteristic geometric design: the (repeated) motif of the sphinx, seated with straight front legs, its wings drawn together at the back, filled with dotted scales drawn schematically but more delicately rounded. Four fringes at the top (typical of the Mycenaean period[103]). The painter Analatos also excelled at depicting the plant motifs also done according to the Mycenaean tradition. At a parallel stage in Corinth the artists present the plant motifs (guilloches, rosettes and palmettes) in their oriental format (Illustration no. 14).[104]

Illustration no. 14
Plant guilloches on an Aryballos (guilloches in the shoulder frieze and rosettes, alongside zigzag lines, in the bottom frieze) and a Proto-Corinthian Kotile (cup) from the beginning of the 7th century BC (according to Boardman 2005:29, figs 28,29).

There began, however, very primarily and rarely, to appear oriental motifs, such as the Tree of Life on Attic vessels. Such as the Proto-Attic Oinochoe from around 700 BC (Plate 16:1) that includes two versions of the motif (alongside the traditional geometric meander). On the lower of the two on the left, there are rosettes with black and white petals and at the end of the stem a long rounded blossom. On the right coiled branches issue from the trunk with buds cleave at the ends. This is no doubt an exceptional and rare description for this period in Athens.

At a later and more advanced stage (end of the 7th – beginning of 6th century BC) of the process of grasping oriental models the Black Figure Style raised the Athenian level to a higher rank and it eventually surpassed Corinth in skill and refinement. The Attic Oinochoe from 600 BC (Plate 11:1) presentation of the figures and the other plant models and especially the sphinxes (as female figures with the famous archaic

smiles) that "mothering" accompany Hermes, receive a refinement and abundant linear details typical of the Black Figures Style. At the same stage in Corinth (on a Pyxis from the beginning of the 6th century BC, (Plate 11:2) there is obvious multiple and dense use of oriental models and motifs, also delicately detailed, however with adherence to the same subjects and composition (of animal and monster processions) without the epic inspiration that typifies the Athenian scene, showing vision and sophistication. There, in Athens, the transition to complex use for expressing mythological scenes and descriptions already exists, such as the famous vessels by the Netos/Nessos painter and many others.[105]

An accelerated process of orientalization commenced in Crete expressed in varied vessels.[106] A Dinos from Arkades (from the mid 7th century BC, Illustration 15 and Plate 29:1-2) with three busts of protruding griffins plastically designed, presents a tangible illustration of the intensive oriental influence (see Illustration no. 16 below concerning griffin heads in metal works).

This expression of combining the vessel surface with sculpture resembles a similar style in Corinth on the "Macmillan" Aryballos body (see also p. 30 and in Appendix 3, p. 47). There is no doubt that the vessels in general, and this vessel in particular, inherited the conceptual design from oriental metal vessels work. However, as said, the ceramic vessel as an object of painting and sculpture, provides a new and different dimension to the metal vessels.

The potter's work, the artistic performance and the complex painting system are very interesting: the bird body of the griffins with outspread wings, painted on the vessel walls, whereas the remaining depiction of the griffin, namely the head and neck, are formed in sculpture. This constitutes an impressive baroque combination. The painter/sculptor received his inspiration from oriental imported vessels. The work on this vessel is reminiscent of a gold bowl from Persia with sculptured additions of lion heads and animal heads in the center of the plates or the bronze trays found in caves on Ida mountain in Crete (for example see Hampe-Simon 1981:171 and Plate 9:1-2) and the combination of griffin and lion heads on a metal Dinos, attached at the base of their necks to the vessel, serving as handles. Many of these bust works were found at Heraion in Samos, on the Acropolis in Athens, in Delphi and Olympia (see further and in note 108).

In between the griffins there are traditional geometric patterns and motifs, and complex plants but in the center

---

[103] The transition of motifs is a subject interesting in itself. For extensive information on the motif see Dessene 1957, Demisch 1977 and see on this subject and the characteristics of this motif as detailed by Crowly 1989:41-46.
[104] See on the process of copying oriental plant motifs in Greece and their expression in Corinth (in this case guilloches) Boardman 1985:78-80, figs. a-b.

[105] Expression of the enriched stage of this process in large vessels (Kraters and Amphoras) ornamentally detailed, particularly in terms of epic report but also oriental motifs rooted in Corinth, went through a process of assimilation and sophistication and moved to Athens, see for example Boardman 1974:figs.5-8.
[106] See Morris 1992:151 (Chap. 6: "Daidalos in Crete") who writes about cults in Crete and the use of oriental funerary customs and others associated with the orient. Her decisive conclusion: orientalization did not in fact cease to visit the island for hundreds of years.

sits a sphinx adorned with a crown (or stylized fringes), wings designed like griffin wings, gathered together and raised. The head and face of the sphinx are somewhat humorously depicted (a smile on the lips, perhaps an archaic smile, typical of the period) that does not coincide with the thunderous calmness on the face, typical of sphinxes.

Illustration no. 15
Dinos from Arkades

The sculptured heads of the griffins, on the other hand, are well depicted as terrifying: the eyes, teeth and open mouth, exactly as the artist expresses the animal's fear of the roaring lion on the Macmillan Aryballos. There, however, the expression is more detailed, delicate and sophisticated. By the way, both vessels have scale shaped decoration (the mane depiction: in Corinth more wavy and less rigid) on the animal/monster necks. This decoration and its location on the neck of the vessel/animal was common in the design of other vessels and these are probably copies of metal vessels that copied oriental models, such as those with griffin heads (from Samos and Olympia see Illustration no. 16 and Plate 30:1-4).[107]

Illustration no. 16
Top: Combination of griffin and lion heads on a Dinos from Olympia, beginning of the 7th century BC (Hampe-Simon 1981: fig.160). Bottom: a bronze Dinos from Samos, first half of the 7th century BC (H-S,164).

The building of a slightly different style system, in the division of decorated area and in the expression of oriental motifs common to the period, but in an interesting combination of the same elements that decorate the head and the neck area of the figural vessel can be found in a prominent example with comparative characteristics,. The Cycladic jug of the mid 7th century BC (Plate 30:5) serve as a worthy and comparative object. The similarity that exists in the decoration of the neck fits the metal griffin from Samos as does the design of the head and the open mouth, design that returns us to the work of the Macmillan painter on the Aryballos we have discussed (see Illustration no. 17 below).

Illustration no. 17
The Cycladic vessel (left), griffin head (handle of the metal Dinos, details from Plate 30) and the Macmillan Aryballos.

Other than the scales motif on the neck and the animal/monster head with the open mouth, attention should be made to the combination of models and motifs, some still according to the geometric tradition, as expressed in the Cycladic jug.

Another vessel from Arkades, Crete (Plate 31:1-2, Illustration no. 18), represents the combination of decoration in its complex, sculptured format and the function purposed by the vessel, which connects us to the style of the previous vessel from Arkades and to the same complexity that exists in the Aryballoi particularly the Macmillan: a small ceramic sculpture from the third quarter of the 7th century BC that shows the kneeling or lying lion motif, holding a perfume vessel in his paws. The tense, closed position of the lion is shown by the threatening open mouth and the folds of the face.

The motif was common in Egypt and the Levant in the traditional format of the completely relaxed lion's position, which appears here differently and may have been done by a local artist. The motif and the vessel (for ritual and/or daily use) were, however, assimilated on the island and developed. [108]

---

[107] See Hampe-Simon 1981:113 who present the discussion on the hypothesis of Hermann (1980) who thought that the vessels from Olympia are local Greek vessels that underwent a local development, alongside the oriental original. There is no dispute among the researchers concerning the oriental origin. The same oriental heritage with these characteristic components continues on into the 6th century BC affecting monumental sculptures. Richter 1974:211ff, figs 296-7 is of the same opinion concerning sculptural style especially of the griffins on which the researcher shows a trend towards delicacy and less monumentalism.

[108] The motif goes through various turning points. For its frequency in the orient and Greece and Crete see Hampe-Simon 1981:279-80 (who raise a discussion for this purpose) and Gehrig-Niemeyer 1990: Kat. Nr. 106, 107 from the 9th and 7th centuries BC. The latter turn the tables in no. 106, probably from north Syria, the lion appears in an aggressive expression whereas the second (no. 107) from Crete (Arkades, probably) it is relaxed. Vessels in this format and for additional purposes (such as salt shakers) achieved a sophisticated and complex expression in ivory works from the Syrian and Phoenician schools

Illustration no. 18
Ceramic sculpture from Arkades. 3rd quarter of 7the century BC
(details from Plate 31:1-2)

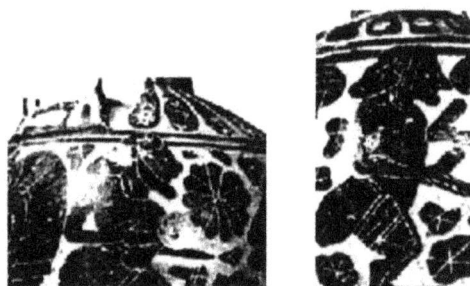

Illustration no. 19
Head of a bearded man made of ivory (relief from the mid 7th century BC) and paintings of "Padded Dancers" on a Lekythos from Corinth and a scene of dancers on Aryballoi belonging to the works of the Welcome Painter (second half of the 7th century BC, according to Amyx 1996: Pls.16,45,1a,2a).

In the discussion on the Potnia Theron motif we have already shown, for comparative purposes, similar works of expression on ceramic vessels, from the Arthemis Orthia temple in Sparta. From the same temple there is (Illustration no. 19) the bearded head made of ivory in relief, from the mid 7th century BC, in impressive miniature (5 cm) work, probably by a local artist (mainly in the design of the hair and together with obvious oriental influences in the design of the male portrait[109]). There is considerable similarity between the male portrait in its present format and the faces of the "Padded Dancers" in the group of Aryballoi and other vessels that came into expression in Corinth during the parallel and following periods (see Aryballos no. 8 and below Illustration no. 19).

It is difficult to find any parallel to this beautiful expression of a face: the large eyes emphasized with brows, the upturned nose, the perfectly designed lips and the pointed beard designed in fine delicate lines, as well as the ear and hair gathered in a coif (?) – so finely detailed, however also in miniature in the paintings of dancers on Aryballoi or other small vessels from Corinth, at some later stages (as said, during the transitional stage and until the late Corinthian period) – for poss comparative similarity.

In addition to the painted ceramic vessels, metal vessel works and monumental sculptural works that loyally present the orientalization phenomenon in Greece – whose specific expression on Aryballoi we are examining and attempting to associate additional works for proper research comparison – there are other typical artistic objects, such as clay and metal works that decorate furnishings or various architectural accessories, In the metal works prominent oriental motifs are expressed in hammering or incising on the bases of relief plates.

In order to exhaust and centralize the components in metal vessel works that influenced and were probably assimilated into various and varied fields of work, such as the work of Aryballoi artists, in terms of style, technique and presentation of decorative subjects – an additional representative work should be shown.

This is one example and one of the most beautiful expressions of the peak of a process during an essential period (parallel to the EC period) and it appears in a wonderful incision on a bronze plate from Olympia dating to the 7th century BC (Plate 19:4, Illustration no. 19[110]): a female griffin feeding a cub, a well known oriental motif[111]. Mention should be made of the two long fringes coming out of the mane reminiscent of the hair fringes element in earlier oriental motifs (in the 9th-10th centuries BC) that traveled westwards.[112]

Do we have here local Greek interpretation of the oriental motif – the griffin enslaved, curbed, tamed or is this purely and simply an oriental version? Through meticulous searching some body items designed in local expression of the Olympian potter may be found, but

during the Iron Age. See Barnett 1982:44 figs 18 a-c. These works have earlier Egyptian origins.
[109] There are examples from sculpture, probably designed by several of the same sculpture groups from Olympia, mostly warriors or riders wearing hats or miters (in sizes ranging between 18 to 22 cm) from the end of 8th century BC and the first half of the 7th century BC, with variations (composition, specific position) from the Phoenician sculpture format. See Hampe-Simon 1981:figs.380-389, 417 and for comparison Labib 1981:11-13, figs.1-3.

[110] On the engraving element and oriental influences on vase painting and other arts in Greece see Boardman 1975a:fig.48 and the parallel at Hampe-Simon 1981:fig.170.
[111] Which developed according to an early Babylonian and Egyptian tradition of the suckling cow and was changed into the suckling goddess (Barnett 1957:143-145, 1982:48) and the development along various planes in the Aegean world during the Minoan-Mycenaean periods, such as the more accepted feeding in the world of griffins-birds. See the depiction of a pair of griffins feeding their young, on an Alabastron from Lefkandi, Euboia from the mid 12th century BC: see Higgins 1997:122, fig. 144.
[112] For handling of the oriental motif and its progression and expression in the Aegean world, according to Crowly 1989:46-53.

there is no doubt that the work derives from a known and fairly common oriental source that appears on the metal vessels we have dealt with and the progression of styles mentioned earlier.

Illustration no. 20
Female griffin suckling a cub. Hammer work on a bronze plate from Olympia, end of the 7ᵗʰ century BC
(Also on Plate 19:4, Boardman 1975a: fig. 48)

A.12 CONCLUSIVE SAMPLING

It is difficult to choose and take one vessel to represent all the many characteristic components mentioned so far. Let us, however, look at the Proto-Corinthian Aryballos from the second half of the 7ᵗʰ century BC (Plate 32:1 friezes spread from top to bottom): all the items and images, including the animals (lions, deer) and the bearded siren[113] are depicted with oriental influence. The same applies for the scene of the dog chasing the rabbit (or hare), a popular scene by all opinions (Boardman 1975a:41, fig. 35). This is a fairly common frieze that reached far way, both in period (appears in the 6ᵗʰ century BC as well) and in expanse (spread to islands such as Rhodes) and for example a Oichonoe from the beginning of the 6ᵗʰ century BC in the "Wild Goat Style" typified by an abundance of oriental motifs (a prominent example see at Boardman 1975a:48, fig. 43). All the above have obvious oriental influence: not only in the selection of subject or motif, but in the transition from describing the figures, at first by the shading method, to emphasize the external outlines, especially by using linear incision to emphasize the items in general, and for figurative expression in particular. In other words there it's clear that there is an emphasis on anatomical details particularly the face according to the practice in working with metal vessels from the east, as seen, for example in the iconographic analysis of several silver and bronze Phoenician plates that represent the origin of the method.[114]

The Proto-Corinthian artistic momentum, or that of the orientalization wave, focuses on a high expression of quality in the miniature works and for the first time brings the experience acquired from the metal vessels and their incision decorations. The artists that adopted the monotonous animal friezes adhered to the Black Figure Style with perfect adaptation. This is the leading idea and the style that characterizes the vessel known as the Chigi Vase (a large Olpe) painted by the Chigi painter, also known by his nickname Macmillan Painter, from the mid 7ᵗʰ century BC. The rich friezes provide scenes of struggles, hunting and a polychrome depiction of animals in a more delicate and improved manner, in terms of skill and daring, compared to vessels until then.

However it is without a doubt that the Proto-Corinthian Aryballos known as "Macmillan" after the same painter, also from the mid 7ᵗʰ century BC achieves a degree of quality that even exceed this larger vessel.

Illustration no. 21
The Macmillan Aryballos (in actual size!)

In many cases the miniature work empowers the skill of the craftsman-potter-painter and uncovers his high talent. In this case they achieved a very high stage and very impressive expression, as Boardman (2002:33) writes: "This is almost the Potter/Painter as Jeweller".

In this case too attention should be made to the rich division of friezes, four on the vessel body, the tiny body of the vessel (6.8 cm and see for example Amyx 1988:Pl. 11a-b).

17 (!) warriors appear in the large central frieze. They are in battle and in complex activity, some falling and some bleeding. Each warrior has a feathered helmet, a spear

---

[113] The earliest Corinthian siren figure – according to Kunze 1931 and Dunbabin 1962:39, Pl. 62, no.1569.
[114] See further concerning the Aryballos and the Phoenician plates. Other representative vessels, such as the early Proto-Corinthian Aryballos at the Ashmolean Museum (1968:12-15.1) see Cook 1977:40; 1988: Pl. 9, A-D and others such as: Demargne 1964: fig.435 and Benson 1989:26 – indicate the significant and valuable connection between the previous silhouette method and the black figures style and the absorption of new motifs. This also states the connection and the

transition between the geometric and archaic periods. Here perhaps the basic most important element: the connection between the historical phenomenon – the ability of the Greek civilized world to absorb, during the transition period, the decisive and significant oriental influences – and the reality that is reflected through the findings. The facts speak for themselves!

and stylish shield. Two additional friezes depicting a horse race and rabbit hunting appear underneath.

Despite the tiny size of the vessel one can see that the figures are proportionally positioned, especially in the central frieze which was accomplished amazingly by the artist. For comparison and to illustrate the momentum of the miniature painting which reached a peak at this stage, a Proto-Corinthian Aryballos from the mid 7th century BC should be presented, double in size (12.39 cm, perhaps a Lekythos[115]) that also combines a sculptured head (owl) and with the subjects and motifs common to the period. The artist's technique in this expression, defined by the catalog (and see footnote 115 below) "Developed polychrome style", probably refers to the advanced stage of the black polychrome technique discussed earlier.

breakthrough the linear boundaries of the frieze, can already be found at a slightly earlier stage to this in its high quality expression. For example the Huntsmen Painter and other painters that created in his style, from the MPC-II (and also see following) that excelled in freely expressing the narrative motif:

Illustration no. 23
The central frieze on the Aryballos associated with the huntsmen painter's style known as Near the Huntsmen painter (according to Amyx 1988:Pl.6, 1a,c,d)

Illustration no. 22
Proto-Corinthian Aryballos (perhaps Lekythos) from the mid 7th century BC (The Norbert Schimmel Collection, no. 50""Ancient Art)

The oriental motifs of the lions and sphinxes presented here in the typical heraldic array are indeed impressive. In addition the interesting work of the artist, potter and painter, who did well in completing the vessel integrally combining the owl head with the potter's wheel work and added the handle and orifice at a later stage.

Still, in my opinion, this work does not compare with the skill, the choice of subjects and the daring expression as well as the conceptual openness of the Macmillan Aryballos artist. All these are expressed in his noncommittal attitude towards the frieze boundaries, as the breaching of these boundaries is done with elegance, in describing the warriors attire and weaponry and their movement above and in the description of the animals below: they break and cross lines in order to cancel the linear rigidity and express a noncommittal connection between the subjects described in the various friezes.

It should be mentioned, that in addition to the combination and description of the narrative components that make the scene attractive, this stylistic development, in terms of openness in positioning the figural groups that

---

[115] See the well known catalog of Norbert Schimmel Collection at the Israel Museum, item no. 50.

B. CORINTH AND THE PHOENICIAN CONNECTION

This chapter intends to encircle the central theme of the work with several surrounding frameworks that include supplementary components, in an attempt to clarify the picture and reinforce the fundamental skeleton of the work. These components are relevant to the central theme, as they relate additional and varied aspects to the final expression in the manufacture of ceramic vessels in Corinth in general and of the Aryballoi in particular.

Alongside the penetration of material influences during the orientalization process, cultural and religious progressions began to take place. Dunbabin, at the time of publishing his well known essay *The Western Greeks*, tried to focus on these processes as well (Dunbabin 1948, 1948b) in order to transfer the weight to the cultural-religious subject and indicate the concentration of oriental elements in Corinth that in his opinion affected the entire process to a great extent.[116] Those used to seeing the Phoenicians everywhere, Dunbabin writes, consider them to have lead the oriental culture to Greece and for them Melikertes, the hero presented in the Isthmus was Melkarth. Dunbabin adds that the source of Aphrodite's rituals and sanctifications is Phoenician, as well as Medea and the Hera Akraia ritual that involved human sacrifices, indicated by the killing of Medea's children – as being Phoenician rituals. The Phoenicians also worshiped Athena known to them as Phoinike, and the month of Phoinikaios was celebrated in Corinth and the Corinthian colonies. These oriental elements, states Dunbabin, are found in higher concentration in Corinth than anywhere else in the Greek world, and initially appeared during the second half of the 8th century, when Corinthian trade began to expand and oriental influences began to appear in Corinthian art.[117]

A remark by Herodotus differentiates the Corinthians as having greater sensitivity and appreciation for craftsmen despite the outward contempt by others and particularly the lakademons, the Spartans (Herodotus II:167).

Previously, Homer expresses a generally negative and hostile opinion of the Phoenicians ("Greedy Scoundrels" *Odyssey* XV:415) but with a mixed reference stating "A silver vase that was the most beautiful in the world because the Talented Daedalic Zidonians made it" (*Iliad* XXIII:740-745), there is an appreciation of the skills of those people identified as traders and craftsmen. Moreover, in the Odyssey, in this reference to their traits and despite their being swindlers, the hero takes advantage of their talents to join their sea voyages in order to reach his destination in safety (*Odyssey* XIII:271 onwards, *Odyssey* XIV:293 onwards).[118]

The ritual enacted in Corinth, the Urania Aphrodite ritual, which became the city-state's official protector, came straight from Phoenicia according to Williams' opinion.[119] Another discussion by Williams on the extensive Stelai complex is interesting in itself. The comparisons to other sites such as Carthage, Cagliari and Nora in Sardinia, and the Phoenician colony of Motya in Sicily – teach of their origin.[120] Moreover, bronze plates (Phiale) found in the layers connected to Stelai Shrine A in the heart of the Corinthian potters' quarter with the incised dedication of τάς Αφροδίτας έμί associate the object to the goddess ritual and once again provide additional information concerning the connection we dealt with between the metal vessels such as the plates at the shrine and our subject. The subject of Stelai, their similarity to the oriental origin and Canaanite source, is of interest to the researchers,[121] as is the location of the finding adjacent to the industrial buildings and potter's workshops, as in the potters' quarter in Corinth.[122]

We have already discussed parallel testimonies of findings of an oriental origin in Crete. On all matters pertaining to the subject of stelai and burial markings like the Phoenician stone cippi or in oriental tradition, it is worthwhile mentioning those recently added from the burial site at Eleutherna. According to Stampolidis (2003) there is no doubt in determining them as Phoenician, probably from the end of the 8th century BC. In any event, the chronological framework determined at this site is between 870 BC to the end of the 6th century BC. There are few Phoenician ceramic findings at the site, but rather varied findings from the orients, such as faience, glass and bronze plates. All in all the findings testify to local pottery manufacture, expressed in the integration of

---

[116] Dunbabin relies and bases his idea on previous studies such as: Farnell 1896 Vol. I:201, Vol. 668, Maass 1903 II:8:257, and see additional bibliography at Morris-Papadopoulos 1998:257.

[117] Even if these oriental elements, as testimony of Phoenician or Syrian settlers, are still controversial, according to Dunbabin, and mainly in light of the relatively small number of Phoenician or North Syrian findings in Corinth itself, it is possible that the Corinthians imported the use of oriental rituals along with the myths, as settlers at the far reaches of the eastern Mediterranean basin such as Al Mina Posideion, see Boardman 1990:169-90, Graham 1986:51-65.

[118] See the hypothesis by Winter 1995:247 (and Morris-Papadopoulos 1998:257-8) concerning Homer's Phoenicians "that do not represent the Phoenician world, but rather represent a sophisticated literary idea, created by him and at the same time acted to create the most extensive social, political, economical and symbolical weave of the ancient Greek state during the archaic period".

[119] Williams 1986:29 refers to the selection of the goddess "that supported the largest and strongest sea faring nation of the time".

[120] Although William doubts the Phoenician origin in Corinth, in Williams volume *Corinth* XV:I,65 and see also the discussion by Morris-Papadopoulos 1998:258.

[121] See carter (1987) for example, who determines that despite the prohibition of Canaanite ritual (and the Israelite according to the extensive reforms by Hezekaya and Yoshiyahu) they were used by the Phoenicians and through them were transferred with various differences to Cyprus and the West Punic.

[122] And as it appears in *Corinth XV:I,65* concerning the group of stelai at Motya which associated with Corinthian ceramics and dated to the end of the 7th century BC and the beginning of the 6th century BC. Morris and Papadopoulos (Morris-Papadopoulos 1998:259) within framework of this adjacent locality, even emphasize the pertinence to the fact that this industry was comprised mostly of foreign settlers (Metoikoi). In this article they add more comparative elements associated with the subject, such as the name associated with the founder of Corinth and the names of the Corinthian colonies and their connection to Phoenician etymology or the trading system and Corinthian ships, the first in Greece, according to sources (Tucidides II 1.13 that were comprised of ships (like the ancient battleships, the triremes) that were constructed according to oriental format.

artistic components characteristic of vessels from Knossos and other centers in Crete as well as on various vessels from productions centers in the Cyclades, Cyprus, Phrygia, the Levantine coast, Attica and Corinth: an expression that typifies the Mediterranean reservoir content, which contains a combination of various cultures.[123]

B.1 ARCHAIC CORINTH

In order to survey the initial development stages of this cultural center, the political moves of the period shall be stated, as well as fundamental elements of construction and religious and public creation that emphasize its importance.

Corinth during the 7th and 8th centuries BC went through dramatic changes. The transition from monarchy to aristocratic oligarchy in the image of the Bacchiadae (king Bacchis family) held by the dynasty in the form of inter-tribal marriages (Endogamies, Herodotus V:92b) although, probably, the manner of government and political management of the monarchy did not change and remained in its previous format.[124] The major impetus of Corinthian colonization that included trade and the distribution of materials and artistic objects, took place under Bacchiadae rule. Syracuse and Korkyra were established by the Bacchiadae and the story on the presence of one of them in Etruria (Demaratos who was deposed by the Tirans[125]) served Ridgway[126] in his study on Pithekoussai.

In the mid 7th century BC rule was passed over to the Tirans (probably through murder of the Bacchiadae king. See Shanks 1999:53, Salmon 1984:190) and Kypselos the Tiran, who was very popular, transferred government by exiling the Bacchiadae, impounding their possessions and even redistributing them, returning exiles and rehabilitating the oligarchy enemies (see Salmon 1984:195, on the exiles at Herodotus 92:V). Kypselos even expanded trade and settlement in the Adriatic colonies (such as in Ambracia, Apollonia, Epidamnus) directed their trade and settlement towards Italy and initiated contact with North Eastern Greece (with its

resources of raw materials such as wood for construction and flowers for the Corinthian perfume industry). During the era of Periander, who succeeded Kypselos, the royal court became the sponsoring center for arts, and sources note Corinth as the origin for temple sculpture and painting, as well as ties with the orient in the Tirans' interest. Thrasyboulos of Miletus re-established friendly ties brought to an end a prolonged period of hostility with the Euboeans on this front and opened routes to the eastern basin of the Mediterranean, as well as ties with Alyattes, King of Lydia (according to Plinius NH:35.6 and Pindar *Olymprian:13.6f*, and the Phrygian and Lydian offerings in the treasury of Kypselos in Delphi – Herodotus I:14). Periander's nephew and successor, for a brief period until the return of the wealthy oligarchic class, was Psammetichos. His name indicates an Egyptian-Pharaoh connection.[127] During this period as well as during the first half of the 6th century BC, the system of trade connections with large centers such as Athens and the Aegina became competitive. Corinthian influence on Athens became substantial expressed in the arts and in other functional frameworks (Murray 1993:151-2).[128] Corinth, besides being an interesting archaic urban center within the context of more massive progression and development in scale of construction,[129] is considered an important and early source for all matters pertaining to temple, public and religious buildings design (Salmon 1984:120-1)[130]. Particularly the system of building roofs and tiles expressed a new and innovative era, and in addition, the architectural ceramic decoration (beginning from the mid third quarter of the 7th century BC), elements used in early Greek temples and other sites and parallel interesting decorations found in Corinthian ceramics such as the Chigi Olpe found in Etruria.[131]

At the beginning of the 8th century BC the temple of Hera Akraia in Perachora on the south eastern side of the Bay of Corinth marks the beginning of the regional building impetus.[132] On this site, in a later ritual building (dining

[123]The Mediterranean international Koiné and the "Multicultural Composition" (referred to by Niemeyer 2003:204) and see Stampolidis 2003:225 and also Stampolidis 2002:330 indicating the importance of trade routes and influential centers of significant Phoenician presence with oriental findings with Cypro-Phoenician features such as: Lefkandi, Attica, Cos, Eluesis, Knossos, caves, Eleutherna, Fortetsa, Idaean. Concerning Lefkandi, Morris & Papdopoulos (1998:262) regard the site as comparable to Corinth and as a more worthy and earlier precedent (see Popham 1980, 1994, Lefkandi:III, 1997), for research on the emergence of dominant influence by traders and settlers from the orient. These centers were places where Greeks and Phoenicians lived together and where a "joint venture" of marketing to the west could develop, the venture on which there article is based.

[124] See Shanks 1999:52 according to Andrews 1956 determination, which questioned any fundamental changes in government characteristics.

[125] See Burkert 1992:23 on the implication of the origin in all matters concerning the accompaniment of craftsmen in his journey to Etruria

[126] Ridgway 1992; 1994 and according to the story of the source: Dionysios of Halikarnassos *Roman Antiquities III.46.3-5*.

[127] For the scholars' opinions concerning institutional changes, the coup in Corinth and the obscurity and anachronism associated with the sources – see Shanks 1999:54-55.

[128] Who also mentions the fact of weight measurement method transfer (in 590 BC) from the Aegina center to Corinth-Murray 1993:151. See also Amyx 1988:675-700 on the progression of Corinthian vessels distribution and the influence as an expression of competition, particularly in the epilog (idem:699-700).

[129] For example the subject of dedicated springs and associated building for pleasure and ritual, see for example Steiner 1992. Salmon regards Corinth, already during the Tiran period, as an urban settlement with buildings for convenience, ritual, economic activity and with a significantly large population, despite the limited evidence (Salmon 1984:80).

[130] Coulton attributes a strong Egyptian influence to the expression of Corinthian temples (Coulton 1977:35-50). On the subject see also Coldstream 1990:68-79, and extensively Johnston 1995.

[131] Murray 1993:152. See for example at Robinson 1984 concerning roof building in the 7th century BC in Corinth and surrounding areas in other Greek temples. Shanks 1999:62 provides the research references associated with the ceramic decoration in those temples built according to the said innovative system.

[132] On the Hera Akraia temple in Perachora see Dunbabin's research and findings on the collection of geometric vessels, and particularly Aryballoi, Dunbabin 1962:9-10.

hall) from the 7[133] century BC, associated with the temple constructed after the Hera Akraia temple, fragments of several temple models were found: small buildings with porticos of geometric design and thatched roofs.[133] Williams (1986:12-14) suggests, in determining the building date, attribution to the rites of Astarte, who is Aphrodite using references of significant ritual items of interest: a figurine from Corinth and a ceramic plate from Perachora describing Aphrodite.[134]

The complex of graves and the system associated with the sacred offerings, not only in temples but of course in the potential layer associated with cemeteries, is perhaps the most significant for all matters pertaining to the artistic discussion relating to ceramic assemblages. As far as we are concerned the discussion is mainly on findings found outside of Corinth (export centers and colonies, the local material was in small quantity). However, pertaining to our subject, in the brief and particular focus on initial development in Corinth it is important to note the facts relating to the trend of changes as the early urban framework emerged in terms of financial resource allocation and their associated symbols and offerings. I shall relate further on to the characteristics and significance of these offerings.

In Corinth tributes placed at burial sites between private dwellings were uncovered, dating back to the 8th century BC. The transfer of these focal points to cemeteries with organized burial lots coincides with the general trend of urban development in a city state such as Corinth.[135] Later, from the mid 8th century BC onwards, cemeteries were established outside of the city. This is a fundamental stage, where focus was moved from the individual grave to public ritual sites. On all matters pertaining to religion, this significant development is also associated with the process of enriching ritual sites and burial systems in public and personal fortunes, where researchers are occupied with the initial development of city states (Snodgrass 1980). Monetary preferences were diverted to these places and these sacred sites played a major role in archaic economy. At this stage inventions and innovative trends in Corinthian art also began to emerge, while the central trend in the ceramic process we are dealing with, i.e. – the transition from geometric to Proto-Corinthian decoration and later to the phenomenal innovation of the orientalization stage, is in my opinion, the determinant one and truly representative of the processes that occurred: the increasing trade, the oriental connections, the urban development and the increased wealth (mainly associated with the nobility and their investments).

B.2 CHARACTERISTICS OF THE CORINTHIAN POTTERY INDUSTRY AND ITS REPRESENTATIVE PERFUME VESSELS

The Corinthian pottery industry, due to the impressive preservation of its products, enabled, more than any other findings associated with Corinth,[136] to determine the fundamentals in local and regional cultural development. Corinthian vessels from the Early and Mid-Geometric period were found in Corinth itself and around Corinthia. During the second Mid geometric period, vessels were exported to Delphi and Attica and during the Late Geometric period that reached centers such as Thera, Dodona and Smyrna (in Asia Minor, in small quantities). At the EPC stage, Corinthian vessels were found in large quantities in many centers of the Greek world, Carthage and Etruria. This distribution achieved the highest level of production and export in relation to other centers in Greece during that same period (Boardman 2001).

As we have seen, at the end of the Late Geometric period and in the transition to the Proto-Corinthian an additional creative stage commenced, parallel to the increasing distribution process. This is the stage of "daring" by the potters and artists in their technical and artistic expression, both in Corinth and within the boundaries of its colonies and in other significant centers (all of which are in my opinion associated with oriental presences, in one way or another, which I will discuss later on). This stage, the orientalization stage, developed in Corinth long before in other Greek centers. During this significant period, production began of vessels that not only served the basic needs of eating and drinking, or ritual, but "upgraded" vessels for functional purposes such as perfume (the Aaryballoi and Alabastrae).

The spherical or globular Aryballoi of the Proto-Corinthian period produced and exported in large quantities belong to this group. This Aryballos, due to its features, is the vessel that shows the process of "vicissitudes and innovations", with their oriental nature within framework of the decorative ideas and applications: the technique (such as incision and color) and the expression – figurative and other varied decorative motifs.

In all matters pertaining to the Aryballoi and their function as perfume vessels, Corinth has been mentioned often due to its perfume industry. Plinius (*HN*:13.5) mentions the longevity of Corinthian perfume popularity. Plutarch (*Timoleon*:14.3), who documented Dionysus of Syracuse in exile, describes him browsing around the perfume stalls of Corinth. At first stage the Aryballoi were delicately made and seemingly, in light of their costly content of perfume oil, were at risk of breakage, however, the state of their reservation is testimony to the

[133] For the attribution between the temple (as in the above models) and the ritual center associated with the ritual dining hall, as researched by Snodgrass, see Shanks 1999:61.
[134] Aphrodite in bisexual format, according to Payne 1940:231-2,Pl. 102, no.183, on these clay figurines of Astarte-Aphrodite see in the summary chapter, page 105.
[135] Morris 1987 researched the early changes in development of the Greek polis, mainly in light of the trends and concepts towards burial and its associated ritual.

[136] On the other hand, see Salmon 1984:117 who detracts somewhat from the role of pottery in all matters pertaining to general production and export capacities, because of the difficulty in monitoring the presence of other products and items.

fact that they were sturdier than they appeared.[137] The findings associated with the perfume industry from the Bronze period in the Aegean expanse testify to an early complex and branched development, in terms of materials, components and their varied functions as well as their trade and transition to various centers by sea.[138]

In the results of scientific tests conducted by researchers as to the contents of ceramic vessels of plastic and figural design manufactured in Corinth during the 7th and 6th centuries BC (closed containers that can be assumed to have contained perfume) several components were discovered testifying to the perfume possibilities and other functions,[139] as designated by written sources (Plinius *HN*:12.62) concerning the materials used at the perfume stores.

This function of the Aryballos as a vessel representing the "alternative" side of daily conduct also challenged the Corinthian potter and artist, to make it very esthetic and more attractive. The factors of the period and the new and opportune variety of oriental components, constituted a stimulatory factor. Therefore, this scale of innovation, as expressed in the Aryballoi development process, is clear and comprehendible. In terms of trade and marketing, as a small perfume vessel along with increasing demand, it most certainly could be stored in large quantities in ship stores and containers. This is an additional rational explanation for choosing it as a very prominent vessel during this period.

B.3 CONDUCT AND MUTUAL INVOLVEMENT IN TRADE

Aubet (1993:72-3) attributes a certain form of conduct to the Phoenicians in times of threat and distress, as a guiding nature, for example, during the siege on Tyre in the time of Tiglath Pileser III (745-727 BC) and during the time of his successor Sargon II (722-705 BC) who besieged the city, their threat was answered by an offering or tax of loaves of gold by the local king (Matan

II). This was the local conduct to maintain complete autonomy where possible, ensure important trade activities and renew contact with the Syrian market in the north after the fall of Damascus in 732 BC. Payment of the regular tax, wherefrom to pave the way to a safe road of commercial and economical freedom, continued over time and characterized the reciprocal system practiced between Assyria and the Phoenician city. Tyre flourished (Ezekiel 26, vs. 27), the wholeness and stability of both parties was maintained and both were positively rewarded according to their individual interests.

The same applies to Phoenician trade practices, which was conducted according to private enterprises by traders who, in return for the initiatives, were given sponsorship and the possibility of freedom and personal and financial autonomy, in places where they were received by various factors of the aristocratic classes with which they came into contact. The palace as a potential financial and trade center, served as an influential trade factor creating contact with the traders. The temples, besides being religious establishments, became "bankers" and in the development of the new settlement of traders and other necessary craftsmen, formed trade unions, the "guilds" that were familial in nature and conducted trade in symbiosis with offerings and tributes at the ritual centers and temples. The silver vase of Achilles mentioned by Homer (Illiad:XXIII:740 onwards) or the keimelia, considered a treasure or preserved element, were such gifts and offerings and not reusable accessories.[140]

B.4 CHARACTERISTICS OF THE KEIMELIA[141] AND THEIR IMPLICATIONS

The merging and blending of artistic styles from various traditions, Syrian-Mesopotamian and Egyptian, processed into a delicate and high quality expression, sometimes even adapted to naturalistic frames, are the elements that characterize the unique achievements of Phoenician art. This blend interested the human friction factors between traders and craftsmen as well as other human components of the peoples with whom they came into contact, thus beginning the impetus and the breakthrough of new approaches, especially on the subject of figurative art.

The impressive expression in these works, for example in ivory and metal, constituted a small portion designed for use by the upper class. These most probably were gifts, offerings and presents, the keimelia, as a gesture of exchange. It should be assumed that most of the material destined for trade arrived at its destination in the form of basic, unprocessed raw material, like the metals (see below), accompanied by the know-how, technique and

---

[137] See the assumption by Shanks 1999:172, who adds and states Payne's contradictory version (Payne 1931:288, Cat.No.486) according to which: these Aryballoi were so delicate so as to be suitable only for the function of containing perfume. Then like today the degree of preservation and storage, in my opinion, is safer, as is the nature of their processing by the potter. Shanks mentions Payne (1931:288) again in connection with the Aryballos found in Sicily (Akrai) which gave off a fragrance when opened. See attainments of Coldstream 1969, 1979:261-2, 1986:324 concerning the production of perfume in Rhodes, Kos and Crete.

[138] Like those found among the remnant of a shipwreck in Ulu Burun, Turkey, at the end of the 14th century BC. See the article by Haldane 1990 on the residues of plants and flowers. The latter suggested, for example, that coriander and pomegranate were used to prepare groundwork oils that stopped bleeding in order to prepare perfume. Several researchers dealt with the subject in this early period: Shelmerdine 1985, Bunimovitz 1987, Knapp 1991. And see the records by Forbes (1965:34) concerning the components of ancient perfumes.

[139] Biers 1995 together with other researchers, as brought by Shanks 1999:173 that also describes the contexts in research concerning cultural symbolism in poetry, according to ancient sources, and all other implications (such as nourishing of the personal spiritual dimension, body pampering and therapy in the source of dedications to gods and the use thereof in all matters pertaining to funerary subjects) associated with the object.

[140] A private enterprise by the traders, but there were also contacts made with the Phoenician ruler on all matters pertaining to the exchange of tributes and offerings and hosting, see Aubet 1996:102-3. On the keimelia, the quality goods of pearls, according to Homer, see Niemeyer 2003:205.

[141] The Homerian term (Odyssey IV:79 "House of Zeus Treasures", IV:91 "Property and treasures", XIX:273 "The Unique Qualities of Glory & Honor" translated by S. Tcharnikhovsky), see Dimock 1995 survey according to the translation by A.T. Murray, and see note 140.

experience in working these materials. Contact with the increasing oriental eclectic multiplicity was also transferred directly through the settlement process of foreigners in the new land. This is probably where the more massive processing and production of materials began, as thus and according to the current situation, there is an obvious shortage of findings in the city state sites of the Levant and a phenomenal lack of any ones of quality.[142] This can be assumed as the conduct of the koiné in the Mediterranean region.

Markoe (2003:211-12) searches for a point of origin even in the material found at Nimrud. The varied and also eclectic material, the features of which were transferred to the west, such as Crete, by artists who arrived there in the same way that they arrived at Nimrud (see B.7 – the import of artists). The influence transferred to local workshops and the slightly rigid style, according to the Egyptian scheme that characterized vessels from Nimrud, was softened and improved in Crete. This is the expression on the metal bowls found in the caves of Mt. Ida and in Eleutherna, which are added to other evidence mentioned earlier in Stampolidis (2003), and which most probably testify to the presence of a Levantine community in Crete in the 8-7th centuries BC. In addition to the bronze vessels there is also quality material imported from the east, such as glass and faience jewelry.[143] This quality material, according to Markoe, did not arrive as import from the Levant, but rather was processed or produced locally by incidental craftsmen or settlers that established a local trading outpost and used local or imported material from Cyprus (Markoe 2003:212). Moreover, in a dramatic breakthrough expressed in the metal material found in western and more remote areas, such as Etruria, in the 7th century BC, also dealt with by Markoe, we can find an additional center for comparison. The expression derived not only from iconographic motifs drawn from the orient, but also in the use of foreign materials, such as ivory and in techniques taken from the east, such as granulation and silver and gold filigree.

The examples from Etruria[144] show the copying of Phoenician models very close to the source, but in

addition there is the copying and development of oriental motifs, while using and processing local raw materials (probably from the silver mines of northern Etruria). From an examination of the samples of vessels from Campania, North Latium and Etruria, there are two style groups that characterize the local material: the one with greater closeness to the source and the second with motifs that have become more naturalist (see note 143) and yet remain oriental in expressive style. The demonic animals such as the sphinx and gryphon have made way for animals such as lions, horses and cows on a pastoral background. The same applies to the figurative scenes of human nature: the figures are earthly, as are the hunting and grazing scenes. The vessels were adapted to local needs, even if manufactured in a Phoenician workshop or one with oriental character and tradition.

The Phoenician or Punic ceramics from North Etruria (from the Etruscan port city of Populonia), also show local activity and production of vessels, mainly for the needs of the aristocratic classes, as gifts or in return for access to the silver mines. From a general comparison of the latter material framework mentioned herein, versus the fact of finding metal bowls (from silver and gilded) found in the graves of nobles that controlled the access to the rich copper deposits in the Trodos mountains of Cyprus – we get a similar picture (Markoe 2003:215).

The three main points that emerge from the comparison made with what was done in Etruria: first, the copying of incidental oriental models adapted through local production, to local codes (the naturalist trend, in this case). Secondly, the use of nearby local raw materials. Its availability expedited production providing the craftsman, potter and artist, whether foreign settler or local artisan, with greater creative freedom – using this acquired knowledge. And finally, on the matter of keimelia, the quality expression achieved simultaneously through local material availability, allowed easy contact with the aristocrat consumer class, paving the way for autonomous freedom in both creativeness and in access to the raw materials and the local mines.

It is very possible that a similar process occurred in Corinth and its surroundings. The Corinthian raw material, in our case, is the flourishing pottery industry. The keimelia, at the initial and significant stage, were the unique miniature vessels of this industry: the spherical Aryballoi, delicate in their form and decorative style.

B.5 CENTERS OF PRESENCE AND INTERACTION

In light of the factual situation pertaining to the scale of findings associated with foreign settlement in western sites, it is difficult to refer to all the subjects raised by researchers: were the Phoenicians only the carriers and shippers of the goods or also those that actually produced these goods? Or did the presence of foreign settlers in

---

[142] On the subject of metal vessels expression see Markoe 1995 (concerning metal vessels not found in the four cities: Arwad, Jebel, Zidon and Tyre) as well as Markoe 2000 and the separation to two ranks of quality on all matters concerning material found in the orient (Nimrud and Iran) also Niemeyer 2003:204, on the iconoclastic element associated with the subject see Moscati 1990:172-7.

[143] See Stampolidis 2002:330-1 on the material at the necropolis in Eleutyherna. Markoe (2203:212) quotes the Homerian source (Odyssey XV:450) as a reference within this context: presentation of the jewelry (necklace) by a Phoenician trader at the palace in Ithaca.

[144] The examples in this case are from Vetulonia (Tomba del Duce), the kotyle vessel is very close in its ornamental style to the Phoenician models. In Populonia as well (gold items attached to an ivory horn from the grave at the necropolis of Podere di San Cerbone), the decorative style is directly associated with the decorative works on Phoenician metal bowls and ivory carving works. In addition, the vessels from Chiusi (silver vessels in local work has prominent Phoenician influence, in the oriental models and in the scene descriptions, especially in the friezes) and the gilded silver bowls from the Etruscan graves from Praeneste and Caere, clearly connected to the Phoenician complexes from Cyprus but with their own local uniqueness (mainly in the

---

expression of plant motifs taken more, and different to the Cyprian corpus, from the naturalist world, and in the figurative plane as well). See Markoe 2003:213-4

fact significantly affect material design? Did this presence have an effect on the local social system and what about the moral impact of their stay? And in terms of time and place, i.e. was it temporary dwelling due to trade, or permanent? Perhaps there was another third factor that transported the influential components from outside, from the Levant to the Aegean and vice versa, etc. (see Stampolidis 2003). As far as I am concerned, the possibility of relating to these subjects through researching expression as perpetuated on the Aryballos examined herein, in other words, the examination of style development components that designate the oriental connection in the full meaning of the word – determines the manner of research on these interesting subjects. By examining the style development process of the Aryballos we are creating a logical and chronological framework. This study, therefore, brings us closer to rationalizing the scale of influence and its movements.

Ancient sources relating to the Phoenicians provide us with a certain situation that emerges through the mention of settlement centers, thereby possible regions of interaction. Homer (*Odyssey* XIII:272-277, XV:415 onwards) refers to the Phoenicians as traders and seamen that landed on the shores of the Aegean on the long journey through the central and west of the Aegean expanse in the Mediterranean, i.e., between Rhodes, the northern shores of Crete and the Cyclades[145] and mentions the commercial activity in Syros (Συρίη) in the Cyclades. Herodotus (I:1[146]; VI:47) Thucydides (VI:2.6, writes about Emporia[147]) and others such as Zenon and Ergias of Rhodes, who are mentioned by Diodorus (V:58) and Athenaeus (VIII:360), state the Phoenician centers of settlements such as in Rhodes (Ialysos[148]), Kythera[149], Thasos and the gold mines according to Herodotus and also those in Thrace according to Plinius and Strabo,[150]

---

[145] Homer attributes them (accidentally or on purpose, in the event of them being phoinikes) to the Mycenaean time period and see Aubet 1996:37ff, 41-5 on the trade policies of Tyre in the 9th century BC and especially the biblical sources, on the establishment of Kition in Cyprus and the great potential of the local copper mines and the naval connection of the Phoenician archaic marine routes and especially all that pertaining to Cyprus and Crete. Also the obvious tendency of Burkert concerning these to centers: "Cyprus and also Crete are in a special position: they have been "orientalizing" all the time" (Burkert 1992:16).

[146] Stating the Phoenician's commercial moves, already at the beginning of the first chapter, when he writes about an earlier period and describes their ships laden with goods from Egypt and Assyria, which often visited the shores of Greece and also mentions Argos as one of the principle centers for docking their ships.

[147] On reference to emporós and its features, see Aubet 1996:104ff beginning with the writings of Homer and Hesiod.

[148] On the interpretation of Kadmos story and the foundation of Poseidon's sacred complex, see the remark by Stampolidis 2003:218, note 5 and see also Burkert 1992:17, n. 15 and the clear proof of perfume production on the island, even before 700 BC.

[149] Herodotus I, 105 mentions the Phoenicians as founders of the Aphrodite rituals there. Interesting in itself is Coldstream 1972:36-7 – the appearance of evidence and remnants of industrial and dying facilities on the island. See also a reference by Markoe (1985:126, n.186) concerning the names of ports (Phoinikous) in Kythera and in other places in South Crete and Messenia.

[150] Herodotus (VI,47) also writes about "the wonderful gold mines in Thasos, that of the Phoenicians" and for that purpose mentions their connection with foundation of the settlement on the island (in the north Aegean Sea, Phoenician Thasos, brother of Kadmos) and about the

Motya in Sicily, according to Diodorus (XVI:48,2;51,1), Malta, Diodorus (V:12,3), the North African colonies – according to Plinius (NH:V,19,76 who marvels at the glory of Tyre in the establishment of colonies such as in Leptis, Utica and Carthage, Sardinia[151] and the Iberian peninsula: Strabo (I:2,3), Plinius (*NH*:19,216) and Diodorus who concludes: "The Phoenicians transferred material from the many and excellent silver mines of the Iberian peninsula to Greece and Asia and to other peoples, because they knew how to work and trade in silver unlike the locals who did not know how to make use of it. In this manner they established their many colonies in Sicily and Sardinia, in Libya and in the Iberian peninsula" – Diodorus (V:35,1-5). "It would appear that they simply knew, already during ancient times, how to make use of their discoveries" (he adds and concludes (V:38,3).

This process, derived from the presence of several factors involved, in these centers, in the friction and merger of the combined potential components within a creative fertile and nourishing framework, is very significant. The Phoenician commercial activities directed at Cyprus, the Cyclades and Crete that took place in the second half of the 9th century BC and very significantly at the end of it,[152] was most probably a significant center of friction as far as we are concerned. Moreover, from the viewing of the other factors surveyed (such as colonial expansion trends of Corinth and the internal and commercial process that emerged) it is possible to understand the push and momentum derived from this friction ("the reciprocal venture" according to Morris and Papadopoulos and the "mutual contact and competition, for example according to Burkert[153]), and which led to the artistic turnabout and breakthrough towards the end of the 8th century BC. On the road leading to the "orientalization" era, the increasing deployment of Phoenician and Corinthian centers towards the central and western Mediterranean only intensifies the process.

Phoenicians who reached the island in their search for Europa (II,44) and who settled there and built a temple to Melqart (or Heracles according to the source) "and did more than the temples built to Heracles by the Greeks". Plinius (*NH*:VII,197) and Strabo (XIV:5,28) refer to the gold and silver mines worked by Kadmos in Thrace on Mount Pangeus.

[151] See Barnett 1987, Moscati 1988, Negbi 1992:609 on Sardinia, and the reference by Aubet 1996:60-4, 135ff, concerning the trade in metals and Phoenician settlement in the 8-7th centuries BC, particularly in Tharros, Sulcis and Nora.

[152] On the initial phase of the route to Ophir during the 10-9th centuries BC and the transition to the second phase, North Syria and Kilikia, and the third - Cyprus and the west (the initiatives derived mainly due to the constraints of supplying goods to the Assyrian empire, which required raw materials such as silver, iron and copper), see Aubet 1996:65ff.

[153] Morris-Papadopoulos 1998:262-3, Burkert 1992:21ff who examine additional factors of mutual contact (not only with the Phoenicians and the afterwards the Euboeans) and particularly the friction in direct intensive contact.

B.6 THE DOUBLE INTEREST: RELATIONS BETWEEN ASSYRIA AND TYRE AND THEIR SIGNIFICANCE

The Assyrian journey by Tiglath-Pileser III across the sea to Syria, Phoenicia and the Land of Israel during the second half of the 8th century BC (734-732 BC) marks the second and important phase of the Assyrian takeover of states and cities in the west (the Levant). Despite Tyre and Hiram II joining the resistance headed by Razin, King of Aram-Damascus, and its capitulation to Assyria, Tyre did not eventually become an Assyrian district (as did the remaining parts of the Phoenician northern shoreline), but continued to pay taxes and recognized the status and sovereignty of Assyria.[154]

The Assyrians preferred to retain Tyre's status as a marine-trading power in order to retain its maritime monopoly. In this case too, it became apparent that partial control and appeasement with the Phoenician ruler at the expense of other countries, would be beneficial for the general policy of the empire and would assist it in retaining its control of other areas.

Assyria's careful politics emphasize the power and importance of Tyre to the region, during a period in which Assyria achieved its maximum expansion westwards. This policy did not fundamentally change throughout the 8th and 7th centuries BC, despite the resoluteness of Saragon II (722-705 BC) and Tyre's decline during the rule of the local King Luli (729-694 BC) and his revolt against Shalmaneser V (727-722 BC), Saragon II and particularly Sanheriv (705-681 BC). The pact form (675-671 BC) between Baal I King of Tyre and the Assyrian Esarhaddon (670-681 BC, Jidejian 1969:468), testifies to the existence of a certain freedom of action in the trade routes in the north and west of the eastern basin of the Mediterranean, unlike in the past, but moderately in light of the Assyrian iron fist policy adopted towards the conquered peoples.

As mentioned, the gradual pressure asserted by the Assyrian rulers over the Phoenician institutional-economic system, caused the bulk of weight to transfer and emphasized the importance of the connection between Tyre and its overseas colonies, in order to establish its hold over these important financial sources. As said, this impetus increased in the 8th century BC[155] and only during the second half of the 7th century BC did Tyre capitulate entirely (approx. 640 BC) becoming an Assyrian province.

Despite the general trend of destroying the other, northern, Phoenician cities, Tyre was not destroyed and even retained its financial and commercial basis in the eastern Mediterranean basin, by establishing a new commercial stronghold in Memphis, Egypt, during 635-

610 BC. The process of Tyre's final fall took place only during the rule of Nebuchadnezzar over Babylon, taking 13 years to conquer the city (585-572 BC) after exiling Atubaal III and the death of his successor Baal II (564 BC). During that period the large Punic colony in Carthage[156] flourished.

According to these political processes and the conduct of the stable mutual interests' status, we can imagine, within the human context, an interesting combination of friction between commercial fluctuations and incessant moving of groups or individuals to new settlement areas, trade centers or other strongholds according to these interests. Researchers dealing with this human mobility[157] enrich the general picture.

B.7 THE IMPORT OF ARTISTS

Especially interesting is the review on the import of talented artists (craftsmen, artisans) from the orient to Corinth and Athens, from the sources: the Demiurgoi, "public workers" according to Homer (Odyssey XVII:383-385). Solon understood the importance of their effectiveness and encouraged the import of immigrant artists to Athens. Diodorus uses the term Technitai that already appears in the framework of Techne by Plutarch (see Burkert 1992:23). Diodorus (Diod.II:43.3) writes about the need to settle (the craftsmen) and release them from taxes, so that as many as possible would arrive and resettle. Within framework of the period this work deals with, the Tirans of Corinth searched for this type of artists to relocate them and make use of their skills. Herodotus II:167,20 states: "Less than all do the Corinthians despise the artisans" and states in relation to those: "those departed from crafts are considered nobles and particularly the Lacedaemons".

According to the periodical political processes mentioned, it should be noted that the migration of craftsmen to foreign places is necessarily associated with the transfer of prisoners and slaves. Reference to researches in this scheme of human mobility has been noted on pages 32. The status of those skilled in crafts was probably better, and they may have been selected for certain works (Homer: Iliad VI:290, XXIII:263 and Odyssey XV:418 and concerning tax releases for craftsmen).

In fact the migration of craftsmen aspiring to move and work in new places in foreign lands was common and not

---

[154] See the survey by Aubet 1996:68-74 on the mutual relationship (details in studies by Oded, Oppenheim, Postgate and others).
[155] See within the context of this period, ivory trade in the Aegean Sea during the 8th century BC and the importance of Phoenician colonies and trading stations, Sakallarakis 1993:345.
[156] See Picard 1969 especially the first chapter. On the artistic expression as surveyed on the subject of terracotta masks see Picard 1969:nos. 9-12, and the catalog by Moscati 1988 on Carthage in general and in the article on figurines and terracotta works in particular see Moscati 1988:328-346. See also reference to Carthage by Aubet 1996:190-200,211-217, and in the bibliography pp. 332-3.
[157] Such as the studies by Zaccagnini 1983, Burkert 1992:41-87 (mainly concerning mobility and migration of craftsmen from the medical profession, various prophets and oracles that arrived from the east) and see recently the subject that emerges within various contexts, such as Markoe 2003:212ff concerning the question of whether there was import of metal vessels at the centers or on-site production and by whom.

problematic in terms of freedom to move between countries, already during the Bronze Age of the east, as shown by Burkert (1992, 23-4) and more so during the orientalization period and later in the west. The same applies to freedom of movement for mercenaries. In terms of artistic expression, we have already seen in the mention of findings at Carchemish and Olympia: the gorgon motif that appears on shields. Other motifs that appeared in Carchemish and Corinth were mentioned earlier. This mobility was possible of course during the orientalization era in the archaic period and no doubt the migration of all these to Greece was facilitated by the increased Phoenician and Corinthian trade activities and in light of the accelerated progress made in shipping and navigation systems.

Further milestones concerning the importance of Corinth according to literary sources: firstly, the location of Corinth, between the Saronic and Corinthian bay, constituted added weight in relating to its international status (Tucidides I:20). The mention by Plinius of the importance of Corinth should also be noted, in his reference to the potters stone in particular and to painting in general (XXXV:15-16, *NH* VII:198).

The examination of artists (potters and painters) names is an interesting subject in itself. I shall mention names such as the Amasis painter or Lydos or Brygos, names of potters and painters from the 6th century BC who probably arrived from Egypt, Lydia or Phrygia. For specific perusal of this subject, it is worthwhile noting the study by Boardman of the Amasis painter (Boardman 1987:141-152).

B.8 THE SUCCESS OF THE "JOINT VENTURE"

It is very probable that the incessant movement of traders and craftsmen between these centers constituted a decisive factor in the success of the Corinthian pottery industry. The success of this "colonial enterprise and of the more extensive trade in the west, was one of the factors that turned Corinth, over a short period of time, from an insignificant city into a leading state in Greece and the first to develop large scale trading and industry". This quote from the article by Dunbabin (1948:18) served Morris and Papadopoulos as a basis for their "Joint Venture" idea.[158]

The Corinthian colonial enterprise constitutes a decisive but not exclusive or even primary fact. However the initial colonial impetus as determined by the Euboeans,[159] does not answer, according to the ceramic findings of this period, the questions asked by the various researchers on

the subjects we are dealing with. In other words, on the issue of the degree of oriental influence during the 8th – 6th centuries BC, the artistic expression as reflected in the Corinthian Aryballoi in particular and other Corinthian ceramic vessels, is extremely unique. In all the aspects I have dealt with and in relation to the subjects raised herein, no other center in this field is comparable.[160]

The quality products, as seen, represent ambition. The large industry of phenomenal scale and with so many quality products such as that of Corinth and in many other centers of Corinthian material, indicate the success of that Oriental-Corinthian venture built of a combination of the two components mentioned: the material components, those incidental to the artist, and the human components that serve the cause, and those in between, the mediators. According to this definition the Phoenicians with their known characteristics on all aspects, most certainly serve as a worthy and suitable human factor.[161]

However, the symbiosis between the Euboeans and the Phoenicians (in the east during the 9th century BC, in the west during a period of mutual activity between 760-700BC, Aubet 1996:286,315) can serve as an example of a joint venture and of the development of mutual interests, and in fact, with precedents of commercial contacts at the end of the 9th century BC (Al Mina and Tell Sukas[162]). However the rich framework of components that characterizes Corinthian ceramics, represents the Phoenician-Corinthian or Oriental-Corinthian joint venture as a unique phenomenon. On all matters pertaining to expression of the phenomenon and its scale and the combination of components in such a dominant creation of Oriental texture within material produced in the west, the Euboean-Phoenician venture cannot compare to this later one of Corinth and the east.

---

[158] This quote comes from the prolog to the article by Morris and Papadopoulos (1998), in their attempt to emphasize the Phoenician contribution to all matters pertaining to the cultural richness of Corinth and particularly its pottery industry.
[159] Ridgway 1992:3, however the manner of the initiative's development was different and the Euboean ceramic vessels ceased to appear during the time following the late Geometric period. See also Morris-Papadopoulos 1998:252. On the Euboean connection see Aubet 1996:314-316.

[160] The orientalization phenomenon during the late geometric period affected Athens and other centers in Greece (Markoe 1996:47ff) but the Corinthian influence in this field, according to the framework of all the components mentioned in this work, was very dominant and penetrated all other centers.
[161] Worthy indeed, as reflected by Morris, on all matters pertaining to the phenomenal Corinthian development locally and particularly its exports, Morris & Papadopoulos 1998:256 and the reference there to Phoenician involvement in the classic case of oriental contribution, in the form of naval experience and concentration of capital, especially from Phoenicia as it appears at Sherratt 1993:361-378.
[162] See Boardman 1985:38-54, 188-133. Boardman (1990) in a newer article on Al Mina, emphasizes the importance of the Greek emporium on site during the 9th-8th centuries BC. Negbi (1992:614) underestimates its value particularly according to the shortage of Greek vessels, such as on other sites in the Levant. See also Waldbaum 1994:53-54. Widening the review on all matters pertaining to Greek ceramic material (mainly Euboean), which began already in the 10th century BC, like those found at Tyre and Ras el-Bassit during an earlier period, cannot reflect any clear picture concerning the Greek settlement centers in the area, but probably can indicate goods passing from place to place and distributed by traders (concerning Tyre see Colstream 1988:39-40, Pls.10:24, 11:45, 12:72-75, and Courbin 1986:175-219 for Bassit). Concerning the above mentioned, by the way, the surprising shortage of Corinthian ceramics from the end of the 7th century BC – beginning of the 6th century BC, at various sites in Israel, see Waldbaum 1994:59. It would appear, according to the current reflection, that stamping the seal on the joint venture is connected to the commercial trend well invested in the west.

B.9 "THE DISTRIBUTION EMISSARY"

The miniature Aryballos, delicate and with outstanding qualities, became the vessel with the highest distribution and most certainly (according to the increasing demand by consumers), served more popular frameworks in the centers it reached and was produced. The general scale of Corinthian pottery distribution was very extensive and it can be assumed that local potters and artists copied and imitated incidental original models.[163]

The questions of whether these vessels arrived from Corinth or the Corinthian expanse, or whether they were produced by new local settlers or by traveling artisans (oriental or Greek) – constitute a research challenge. According to the artistic analysis of the Aryballos components we have the features of the finished product, i.e., all the oriental components transferred to the creative environment and assimilated by one way or another, into the material we have, and which appears in every corner of the Mediterranean basin. All these, in fact, serve as witness to the success of that joint venture where the Aryballos, as the "distribution emissary", heralds the new phenomenon.

In the process of producing pots in Corinth during the period discussed, there were several stages. At first the Corinthian pottery presented the continuity of production components, mainly the design with the traditional features and with digression to several foreign factors. The more complex combination was not late in coming and constituted a decisive factor. It symbolized the cultural meeting and with such innovation that transferred the esthetic turnabout into one direction. Focus was also converted to the new center. In these terms, Burkert's title "The Orientalizing Revolution" (1992) is indeed worthy. There is no doubt that the decisive meeting occurred from the friction of several factors and the mutual participation of interests. For example, the cooperation between the potter and consumer factors that appreciated the new qualities, led to new impetus and acceleration. There were no conflict of interests but heterogeneous activity such as the exchange of gifts and offerings, and other features of commercial activity already mentioned. According to Shanks (1999:206) this heterogeneous phenomenon is sufficient, and therefore there is no need to delve into the question of who was responsible for transferring the goods and what is the center of influence. The Cauldron, symbolically, contained a mixture of different cultures, and the Mediterranean basin was such a cauldron. The colonies, in terms of population composition, comprised of Greeks and settlers and were not a homogenous body. It is difficult, as I have already

mentioned, to relate to and determine the responsibility of factors (especially according to circumstance and in the absence of weighty evidence or the shortage of findings) to historical moves. Presentation of the heterogeneous fact is indeed worthy, however the most clear and cutting fact as far as I am concerned is the infiltration of oriental components to Greek culture in general, and to Corinth in particular, during defined periods and in the manner as expressed in local ceramic creations. This fact in itself is indicative of an outstanding and "revolutionary" phenomenon. As far as I am concerned, the vessel through which these important changes and improvements can be examined and which constitutes the best representative of this phenomenon is the Aryballos.

---

[163] On the scale of distribution see the summarized and comprehensive information by Amyx 1988:675-700, on the problem of identifying the "influence" (as a problematic term) and model imitation see Amyx 1988:678ff and particularly the epilog 699-670. In stating the quantity of sub-geometric Aryballoi (Proto-Corinthian) by Neeft 1987:11-12 we can conceive the distribution framework, as from a survey of the total framework of evidence from the Greek colonies – Neeft 1987:363ff (together with the attempt at dating which does not necessarily coincide with the date of the colonies establishment, for example in Taranto).

The Mediterranean Basin

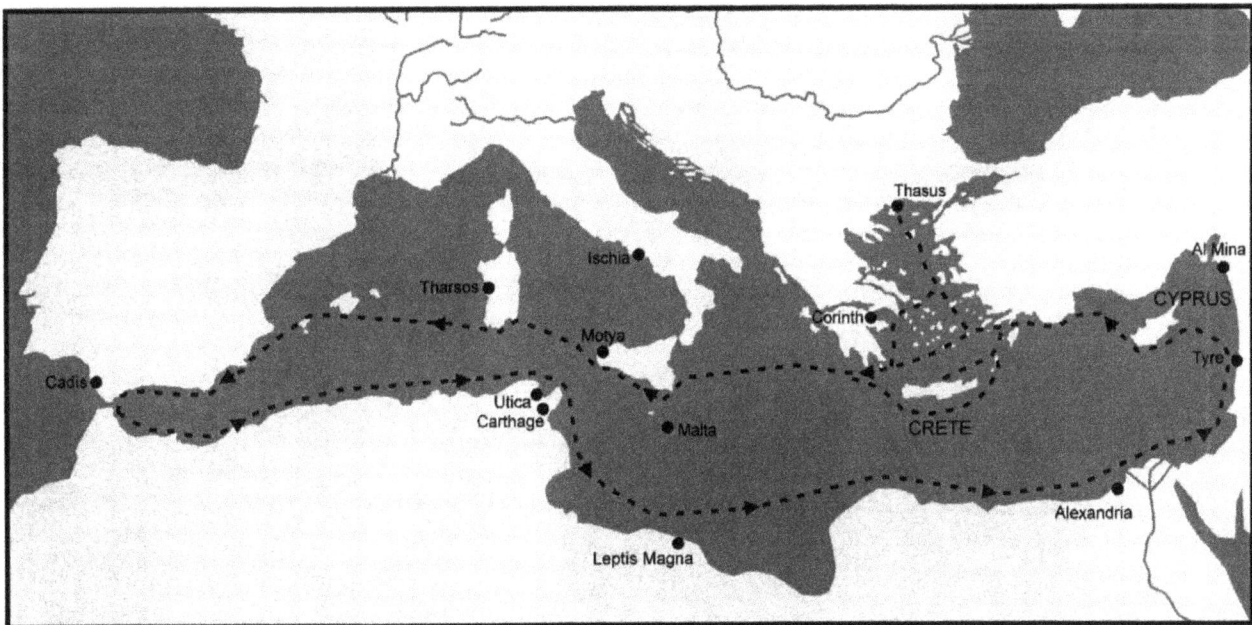

Phoenician shipping routes in the Mediterranean Basin

41

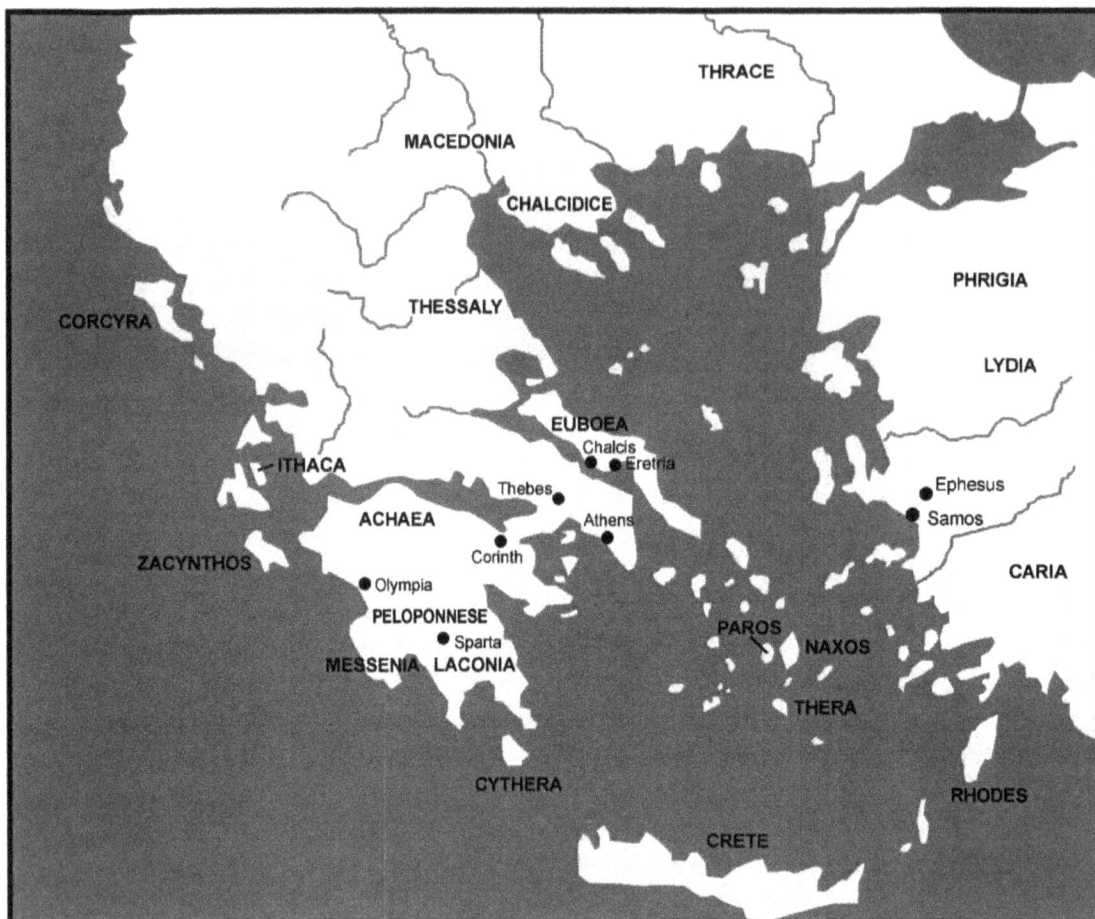

Corinth and the Aegean Expanse (according to Murray 1993)

C. SUMMARY

Walter Burkert in his book "The Orientalizing Revolution" sums up the importance of the archeological findings discovered in Greece during the archaic period in a single sentence: "It is not Greek texts, but rather archaeological finds which offer a solid foundation for tracing Eastern cultural influences in Greece in the eighth and early seventh centuries and for evaluating their significance" (Burkert 1992:14).

John Boardman (Boardman 1985:74) emphasizes the importance the oriental influence expression gave to the ceramic material in Greece more than any other medium: "In Greek work the medium which tells us most about the way the artist used oriental motifs is not the one in which they were ever much employed in the east (for instance in the design of clothing and other fabrics) but vase painting". The ceramic matter we dealt with in this work leaves clear and weighty traces that belong to the process of oriental influence on Greek culture.

We can now summarize several points that represent the subject of this work with emphasis on characteristics of the potters' work and the painters' art on the Aryballos from the archaic period in Corinth:

- The Corinthian Aryballoi were small in size particularly compared to Attic vessels, or even Argives (Argos). The best quality and most excellent work of the Corinthian painters is expressed on small vessels such as the spherical and rotund Aryballoi.

- These quality vessels which were designed for a clear functional purpose, became a very popular export particularly during the Proto-Corinthian and the early Corinthian period. The vessel, which over the years became "the number one export material" of Corinth to the east, as testified by the finding discovered at sites such as Al-Mina and Naucratis, as well as at Dor, Mesad Hashavyahu, Ashkelon and others – could definitely have provided for the high local demand (according to their life styles over hundreds of years).

- The Aryballoi appeared in new, adventurous artistic expression, experimental to a large extent, which was unprecedented. Coldstream, who researched and surveyed development of the decorations (fauna and flora) taken from the oriental lexicon, mentions a Proto-Corinthian Aryballos from 700 BC, which clearly indicates the stylish developments according to the beginning of incision attempts and outlining the way towards the Black Figure Style.

- A more spontaneous and free performance of the new components lead to an artistic breakthrough. Inspired by the oriental motifs, potters and artists allowed themselves the natural freedom to develop and express themselves.

- The vase painting includes the oriental Potnia Theron/Artemis motif that was especially common in Corinth during the archaic period. It is reinforced in light of the fact that painting of the Greek gods and goddesses was poor on vessels from Corinth compared to relatively extensive painting on Attic ceramic material. Moreover, the combined significance derived from this specific motif together with the appearance of other associated motifs, such as the Frauen Festival and the padded Dancers and in addition to the fact that these scenes appeared at a time of multiplied consumption of Aryballos vessels – are testimony to its importance as the most popular vessel during the orientalizing period and perhaps even indicates some local ritual inspired by the orient of greater value than other rituals. Indirectly this indicates a plausible possibility of settlement by traders or other settlers from the east. In any event, the center of local perfume oil manufacture may reinforce this opinion.

On all matters pertaining to goddess ritual in Corinth and its oriental origins and the connection between this center to its origins in Crete: clay figurines made in molds, a technique taken from Mesopotamia and Syria, appear in Gortyn, Crete, and in Corinth at around 700 BC, as was mentioned in the chapter dealing with the Potnia Theron motif: the expression of Astarte-Aphrodite on clay plates is probably of Syrian origin. The local Greeks adopted the oriental model and adapted it to the local deity.

- As for the subject of Phoenician metal plates and bowls: Boardman's reference to the development of early pottery in Greece and to the process of absorbing oriental motifs from the metal material and from oriental ivory works, states as follows:
"In decoration of pottery there were considerable changes as a result of observation of Eastern decorative forms. These were to be observed not on Eastern pottery but on bronzes and ivories, many of which were decorated by incision or in low relief with figures far more detailed than the black Greek geometric silhouettes." (Boardman 2001:31).

Now, after having examined the characteristics of the Aryballoi vessels and other accessory objects in the process that occurred during the course of the period discussed in this work, the transition from the silhouette style of the geometric period to the Black Figure Style and the black polychrome technique is far more clear and comprehendible.

Other than the analysis of the decorative framework and its implications, the function served by the metal object should be mentioned: a vessel of offering adapted to Greek requirements, as seen later in the Greek Phiale. Thus, via that same local functional demand, use began of the Aryballos vessel for perfume oils.

The decorative framework of these vessels which came as a comparison, includes the technical processing style of the vessel, i.e., the incision that emphasizes external outlines and internal features (anatomical in the figural descriptions), and also includes the motifs and items that characterize the vessels and their transfer, in this oriental format, to ceramic vessels in general and to the delicate craftsmanship, in many cases, on aryballoi vessels in particular.

Mainly, at the peak of transferred skills, lies the integration of the incision technique for extra delicate emphasis of the silhouette style. This is a decisive factor in the establishment of the black polychrome technique and the Black Figure Style that characterizes the Aryballoi throughout the periods dealt with in this work.

Examining the subject of metal plates provides a wider point of view concerning the subject of motif and iconographic components transfer such as those that exist in the oriental Syrian-Hittite, the Ugarit (on Plate 27:3 – an interesting precedent of a gold plate from the 15th-14th centuries BC) and the Phoenician traditions, that precede and parallel our period.

Other than the incision method which, as said, researchers indicate as a principle expression of an earlier source in metal and ivory vessels, the wide frame that includes the various decorative subjects of motifs and specific scenes, are added. The attractive Aryballos vessel, both functionally and artistically, demonstrates the best of the styles acquired from these oriental vessels.

- One of the important conclusions from the work is connected to Phoenician trade and its implications. It is possible that trade was run according to private initiatives by traders who created individual frameworks and personal freedom, such as on the matter of barter or in providing gifts and receiving favors in return from the aristocratic class, perhaps on the background of their settling in a new place or their attempt to assimilate within the local population, however not only through trade initiatives but through the attempt to use their skills in order to receive legitimization for their continued existence in the place. There may also have been initiatives of a political nature or a wider, more "global" interest by a ruler in the parent country. As a result of continued pressures exerted by the dominance of a power such as Assyria on the Levant, new directions and more and varied initiatives may have been created in the attempt to finance the state under pressure and of course the continued demands of the conquering power.

- According to the data in my research, it can be assumed that conduct between factors had the nature of a joint venture or mutual competition derived from the centers of contact and friction that fed the creating factors, and yielded, in any event, good results. As seen, it is difficult to measure the degree of interaction between the Phoenicians and Corinth in their commercial conduct and in light of their settlement trends. Yet according to the facts in the field, does it matter if the scope of Phoenician trade was greater than the welcome initiatives of Corinthian traders? Not necessarily. The visual expression on Corinthian vessels is that which undoubtedly reflects the degree of oriental influence and the dominance of the absorption and processing of oriental motifs.

- A new era emerged at the center of urban development in Corinth: the transfer of burial plots to public burial sites, the construction and enrichment of ritual sites and temples that became a central and substantial part of the archaic economy and the integration of innovative elements in construction, architecture and ceramic decoration. All these integrated with a single increasing cultural framework, represented also by the transition stage in ceramic design and Corinthian pottery decoration. In this process, the geometric stage transferred these traditions to the renewed Proto-Corinthian in a richness of detail, but it was mainly the conceptual stimulation of oriental elements that caused the complex and interesting emergence of that era. This is the orientalizing era, and from this overflow of creativity and the current flow of momentum, I retrieved the chosen vessel, the Aryballos.

APPENDIX 1. ADDITIONAL ORIENTAL MOTIFS IN THE CORINTHIAN POTTERY

In all matters pertaining to the copying or enhancing of typically oriental motifs and models that appear on Corinthian vessels, the following data should be specifically stated and added:

A. In figurative painting: the lion figure from the neo-Hittite art (with the squiggly tongue) appears similarly in Corinth. After the mid 7th century BC the Assyrian type of lion appears with its sharp nose, folded ear and thick mane. It gets a local Corinthian nature. In the painting of the shoulders of lions and other animals in the 7th century BC, the specific technical term known as "boxed-in" appears amongst many animals mainly in the Neo-Hittite art as well as the Assyrian, (Boardman 1985:76, fig. 23b,d,e and all other samples and nuances should be examined using his meticulous diagnosis). As we have already seen (illustration no. 4b) in the frieze of the Proto-Corinthian Aryballos vessel: the figure of the lion with the additional human head that emerges from its back appears in the orient on a stone relief from Carchemish.

B. Demonic and monstrous figures, most of which are taken from the oriental reservoir or from that same Mediterranean cauldron that combines varied items and motifs dealt with in previous chapters: such as sphinxes, griffins, the chimaera, the siren and the gorgon that already appeared during the Bronze Period in Greek art, during the Archaic Period went through a process of increasing use with a special emphasis on the ceramic material in general and particularly that of Corinth. The figure of Triton should also be added: the half man half fish that originated from Assyria or in a different format of Neo-Hittite art, which appears in an interesting version on a Corinthian vase (Boardman 1985, 77, fig 25a).

C. Sophisticated plant combinations imitate the oriental Tree of Life motif (with twirling branches and palmette endings), a popular motif which, in its local application, transited to a combination that divides and centralizes heraldic groups in Corinthian vessels. The lotus motif, that we have mentioned and discussed throughout the paper, is expressed in its oriental format but also more abstractly, such as in the characteristic rays motif. Another common oriental motif is the rosettes which are used, in general, to fill in space.

The oriental plant motifs did not break the geometric decorative pattern to which the Greek artists were accustomed, and indeed the artists prolonged this decorative tradition. However, once having experienced the profusion of new components, they enriched their lexicon, and in many cases "pasted" or copied, using their experience and skill, these components to the previous patterns. This was, as said, the common use of the lotus and palmette patterns and the popular rays decoration that was given new variations and changes according to the "veteran" geometric formula or in a different format.

APPENDIX 2. ENRICHING THE CORINTHIAN ARTISTIC FRAMEWORK AND ITS IMPLICATIONS

The decorative pattern of the plant designs together with the groups of figural motifs, such as with the animals first and later the human figures, which had appeared long before in the orient, began– especially at the end of the geometric period and the beginning of the early Proto-Corinthian period, sometimes with an accelerated process in the MPC II and LPC periods - to gradually replace the parallel place in local patterns. As a result the scenes began to be enriched. More significant and discernable differences appeared, such as between the genders and the stating of details associated with divine figures, such as clothing and other accessories. Especially prominent is the positioning of the traditional attributes to the traditional Potnia Theron figure, the local Artemis. These attributes are associated with a common oriental motif: its specific presentation, i.e., her pose and grasp of the various animals.

Other motifs and subjects that appear in the oriental scene, such as wars, struggles, journeys, victory processions and offerings as well as hunting activities, came into widespread use in favor of Greek mythological and epic scenes. The tradition of victory and offering processions, transferred from the orient, flourish, for instance, in the ivory works from the late Bronze age (see discussion at Leibowitz on the Megiddo ivories. Liebowitz 1987:19). Emphasis should be given to the description that appears on another early example of a decorated ivory plate from Megiddo (dated from the 13th century BC, Markoe 1990:18-19). It brings tidings of some of the characteristics that appear within the framework of the period discussed in this paper. Its making was based on similar styles from Egyptian wall reliefs or miniature art works: the victory procession of a ruler returning from a military conflict as well as seated on his throne welcoming the royal delegation bearing gifts. The work is characteristic of the Egyptian tradition but was done according to local iconographic tradition with emphasis on the narrative. An interesting combination exists in the use of well known motifs from Egypt and at the same, probably through the accumulated experience of the local artist, high quality expression in the local Canaanite incision work.

These characteristics appear later in the periods between the 8-6th centuries BC. Glen Markoe in his survey of the motif absorption and assimilation process on Phoenician metal bowls and plates, focuses on the process, expressions of which were transferred to Greece (Markoe 1985:91ff). We find these motifs in the ivory works and other works of Phoenician export (Markoe 1990:18-22, in his reference to the art work associated with the sarcophagus of Ahiram, probably from the beginning of the 12th century BC). In all matters pertaining to local Corinthian expression (as well as in other colonies and centers) during the periods discussed in this paper, the process gains momentum and even climaxes. These subjects and scenes appear already in the mid 8th century BC and perhaps even earlier, and in the words of

Ahlberg: "Geometric artists were inspired by North Syrian and Assyrian art in their scenes from the real world, especially pictures of fighting." (Ahlberg-Cornell 1992:180). The expressions of epic scenes on the Aryballoi included in Ahlberg's plates are no less impressive (Ahlberg 1992: fig. 78, 88-99, 115, 1229) as well as a vessel examined here, which belongs to a style resembling that of the Hunters painter (Ahlberg 1992:fig. 272a).

Naturally, the ceramic vessel in general and the Aryballos in particular became a sort of medium for transferring the narrative message and for presenting the artist's personal interpretation of daily life, religion and the belief in gods. This quality vessel very soon became accessible and popular on the markets for any demand, thereby transferring the message as a source of extensive visual information. The effectiveness of the message transfer, in terms of communication, was greater than any written text which was less accessible to local communities. There is no doubt that the Aryballos with all the components and characteristics mentioned here, became an important medium for the transfer of these messages and ideas, from the outset of the process, with its unique and quality expression. Its contribution, therefore, is significant in terms of the material and cultural components that affected periodical changes of obvious value.

APPENDIX 3. "THE DAEDALIC PHENOMENON"

In Crete, as a center of intensive oriental influence, the oriental style was exhausted into what is known by several researchers as the "Daedalic Phenomenon" (Boardman 1975a:57ff and particularly Morris 1992 in her remarks on the subject researched in her book in chapter 6: The "Daedalic" Style, and its association with the style on Proto-Corinthian Aryballoi with figural heads by researcher Jenkins). Daedalism is defined as a technique acquired from the east and given expression mainly in Cretan art: the use of molds to create plates and sculptural figures such as clay figurines. Production became mass with characteristics typical to this style, especially in the design of the faces of the various figures. The type substantially resembles the design on sculptural plates that describe the eastern goddess Astarte usually depicted naked. In Greece the type was copied and dressed and the goddess was named Aphrodite. The facial features were changed and adapted to the local Greek types, i.e. – sharper and more alert features in their expression differing from the oriental rounded faces and pudgy figures.

The Daedalic type appeared in metal works, for example the Kriophorus motif that appears on a bronze Cretan statuette from the last quarter of the 7th century BC (Plate 33:1) that expresses a process already indicating the integration of the Daedalic oriental head with Cretan attire. The same applies to a bronze statuette from the third quarter of the 7th century BC from Thebes (Plate 33:1). In stone sculpture there is the well known Auxerre Goddess (approx. 630 BC) which combines Daedalic

sculpturing characteristics and attire, particularly that covering the shoulders, with local Cretan style.

Interesting in themselves are the stone reliefs from various places in Greece such as the one from the acropolis in Mycenae in Cretan-Oriental style from around 630 BC (Plate 34:4) and the relief from Malesina in Boeotia, from the end of the 7th century BC (Plate 34:5) which describes in provincial Daedalic style, the head of a woman in the well known Oriental style of the "woman in the window" that appears in Phoenician style ivory works (panels) from Nimrud from the 9th century BC (Plate 34:1-3). An interesting survey of the motif was conducted by Barnett (Barnett 1957:145-151, Pls. IV, C12, C14-15) who expanded the discussion to Phoenician ivory works as well. The Daedalic style appeared also on individual items or works that include several joint components, such as in jewelry, expressed in the miniature and quality work to which characteristics we were introduced in previous examples, as well as in the creation of figurative Aryballoi and their accompanying paintings.

A gold piece of jewelry, probably from the island of Melos, from the second half of the 7th century BC expresses the quality of this work: human heads in Daedalic style, as well as bulls and bees, are drawn on petals, in an original and even somewhat amusing variety. The human heads (with their familiar archaic smile) are facing outwards forming a connection with the viewer and in coordination with the plant petals, while the animals appear in frontal formats. At this developmental stage, the sophistication and daring so delicately expressed, have parallels, but none reach this height of achievement. Please note the granulation style decorates and refines the leaves and especially the archaic young heads and the bulls heads.

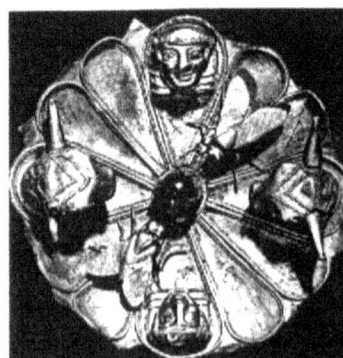

A piece of gold jewelry from Melos(?), second half of 7th century BC (Boardman 1975:fig. 51)

There are sculptural groups that decorate and ornament the temples where the figures appear sitting and standing, alternatively, as can be seen in the various stone relief works and in the gravestones at Prinias (which include figures engraved in the soft stone that are characteristic of metal) in Crete from the 7th century BC. Morris speaks about works done in Prinias and associates the finding discovered there with early Levantine art works (Morris 1992:145, n. 192, 155-1599, 163, 165).

Work by the Macmillan painter on the Proto-Corinthian Aryballos from Thebes at mid 7th century BC can serve as a mediatory vessel and a worthy means for examining the last subject we dealt with, i.e., the connection to the "Daedalic Phenomenon" and its significance for the subject of this paper in all matters pertaining to the Proto-Corinthian Aryballoi.

The Aryballos with the youth's head in this style (Daedalic or archaic see p. 10, the Aryballos of Berlin) does in fact sum up most of the components of this work: exhaustion of the artistic features and qualities of the specific vessel, which were discussed in detail within framework of the artistic analysis.

Proto-Corinthian Aryballos from Thebes. Work by Painter
"Macmillan", mid 7th century BC
(According to VA IZOA Greek Art, Sheldon Nodelman)

CHRONOLOGICAL TABLES

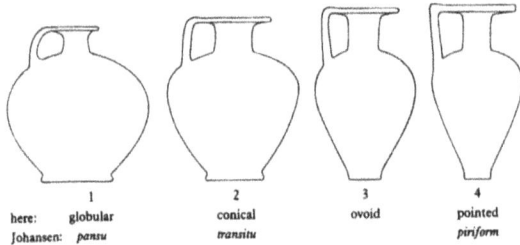

1	2	3	4
here: globular	conical	ovoid	pointed
Johansen: *pansu*	*transitu*		*piriform*

The Proto-Corinthian Aryballoi (according to Neeft 1987:33)

THE PROTO-CORINTHIAN ARYBALLOS[164]

The Period	In years BC	
Early	715-700	
Middle	700-685	Globular Period
Late	685-675	
Latest	675-670/665	
Early	680-675	
Middle	675-670	Conical Period
Late	670-665	
	665-640/635-625	Transitional Period
Earliest	665-660	
Early	660-650	
Middle	650-640	Ovoid Period
Late	640-630	
Latest	630-620	

THE ARCHAIC CORINTHIAN PERIOD [165]

Late Geometric: Up until around	725 BC
Early Proto-Corinthian	725-700
Middle Proto-Corinthian I	700-675
Middle Proto-Corinthian II	675-650
Late Proto-Corinthian	650-640
Transitional	640-625
Early Corinthian	625-600
Middle Corinthian	600-575
Late Corinthian I	575-550
Late Corinthian II	550 →

Additional version[166]:

Late Geometric[167]	750-720
Early Proto-Corinthian	720-690
Middle Proto-Corinthian I	690-670
Middle Proto-Corinthian II	670-650
Late Proto-Corinthian	650-630
Transitional	630-620/615
Early Corinthian	620/615-595/590
Middle Corinthian	595/590-570
Late Corinthian I	570-550
Late Corinthian II	550 →

---

[164] According to Neeft 1987:33 (and see chapter dealing with the subject: Absolute Chronology and his conclusions ibid, on page 397).

[165] According to Payne 1931 and according to Dunbabin 1962 (Perachora II,6).
[166] According to Amyx 1988.
[167] Beginning of dating also according to Coldstream 1968, 1977.

BIBLIOGRAPHY

All sources cited in this work are taken from the Leob series, unless stated otherwise.

Sources

Athenaeus: *The Deipnosophists*. Transl. by C.B. Gulick in 7 vols. Loeb (1927-1941).
Diodorus Siculus: *Library of History*. Transl. by C.H. Oldfather, C.L. Sherman, C.B. Wells, R.M. Geer in 12 vols. Loeb (1933-1967).
Herodotus: *The Persian Wars*. Transl. by A.D. Godley in 4 vols. Loeb (1920-1925).
Herodotus: B. Shimron & R. Zelnick-Abramovitch, *Herodotus*, Papirus, Tel Aviv University, 1998 (Hebrew).
Hesiod: Transl. by H.G. Evelyn White. Loeb (1914).
Homer: *Iliad*. Transl. by A.T. Murray, revised by W.F.Wyatt in 2 vols. Loeb (1999).
Homer: *Odyssey*. Transl. by A.T. Murray, revised by G.E. Dimock in 2 vols. Loeb (1995).
Homer: *Iliad, Odyssey*, Transl. S. Tchernichowsky, Am Oved, 2001 (Hebrew).
Pindarus: *Olympian odes, Pythian odes*. Transl. by W.H. Race. Loeb (1997).
Plinius: *Naturalis Historiae*. Ed. C. Mayhoff. Teubner, Stuttgart (1899-1906. Repr. 1967-1970).
Plutarch: *Parallel Lives*. Transl. by B. Perrin in 11 vols. Loeb (1914-1926).
Strabo: *Geography*. Transl. by H.L. Jones in 8 vols. Loeb (1917-1932).
Thucydides: *History of the Peloponnesian War*. Transl. by F.C. Smith in 4 vols. Loeb (1919-1923).

Books and Articles

Acquaro, F. 1985. "La Sardegna fenicia e punica: fra storia e archeologia". *Bolletino d'Arte* 31-32:49-56.
Adams, L. 1978. *Orienalizing Sculpture in Soft Limestone from Crete and Mainland Greece*. British Archaeological Reports, International Series 42. Oxford.
Ahlberg-Cornell, G. 1967. "A Late Geometric Grave-Scene Influenced by North Syrian Art". *Opuscula Atheniensia* 7:177-186.
- 1992. *Myth and Epos in Early Greek Art, Representation and Interpretation*. Jonsered.
Akurgal, E. 1966. *The Art of Greece: Its Origins in the Mediterranean and Near East*. New York.
- 1968. *The Birth of Greek Art. The Mediterranean and the Near East*. London.
Albright, W.F. 1941. "New Light on the Early History on Phoenician Colonization". *BASOR* 83:14-22.
- 1950. "Some Oriental Glosses on the Homeric Problem". *AJA* 54, 162-176.
- 1958. "Was the Age of Solomon without Monumental Art?" *Eretz Israel* 5:1-9.
- 1960. *The Archaeology of Palestine*. Rev. ed. Middlesex.
- 1961. *The Bible and the Ancient Near East*. New York.
- 1966. "The Amarna Letters from Palestine, Syria, the Philistines and Phoenicia". *The Cambridge Ancient History*: Vol. 2, Chap. 20, 33.
Aldred, C. 1971. *Jewels of the Pharaos*. London
- 1975. "Egypt: The Amarna Period and the End of the Eighteenth Dynasty". *The Cambridge Ancient History* II:Ch. 19.
Amyx, D.A. & Lawrence, P. 1975. *Corinth* VII: 2, *Archaic Corinthian Pottery and The Analoga Well*. Princeton.
- 1988. Corinthian Vase Painting of the Archaic Period. Vol. I-III, California.
- 1996. "Studies in Archaic Corinthian Vase Painting". *Hesperia: Supplement 28*.
Andrews, A. 1956. *The Greek Tyrants*. London.
Arias, P.E. & Hirmer, M. 1962. *A History of Greek Vase Painting*. London.
Artzy, M. 1998. "Roots, Trade, Boats and "Nomads of the Sea". In: Eds. S. Gittin, A. Mazar & E. Stern, *Mediterranean Peoples in Transition' 13ᵗʰ to Early 10ᵗʰ Cents. BCE* 439-448. Jerusalem.
- 2001. "White Slip Ware for Export? The Economics of Production". In: Ed. V. Karageorghis, *The White Slip Ware of Late Bronze Age Cyprus*. Proceedings of an International Conference (Nicosia). Wien:107-115.
Astour, M.C. 1965. "Greek Names in the Semitic World and Semitic Names in the Greek World". *JNES* 24:346-350.
- 1967. *Hellenosemitica. An Ethnic and Cultural Study in West Semitic Impact on Mycenaean Greece*. Leiden.
Aubet, M.E. 1996. *The Phoenicians and the West. Politics, Colonies and Trade*. Cambridge.
Austin, M.M. 1970. *Greece and Egypt in the Archaic Age. Proceedings of the Cambridge Philological Society: Suppl. 2*. Cambridge.
Baramaki, D. 1961. *Phoenicia and the Phoenicians*. Beirut.
- 1967. *The Archaeological Museum of the American University of Beirut*. Beirut.
Barnett, R.D. 1948. "Early Greek and Oriental Ivories", *JHS* 68:1-25.
- 1956. "Ancient Oriental Influence on Archaic Greece". In: Ed. S. Weinberg, *The Aegean and the Near East*. Studies Presented to H.Goldman:212-238. New York.
- 1956. "Phoenicia and the Ivory Trade". *Archaeology* 9, 2:87-97.
- 1957. *A catalogue of the Nimrud Ivories, with other examples of Ancient Near Eastern Ivories in the British Museum*. London.

- 1958. "Early Shipping in the Near East". *Antiquity* XXXII no.128:220-230.

Barnett, R.D. & Wiseman, D.J. 1960. *Fifty Masterpieces of Ancient Near Eastern Art.* London.

- 1969. "The Sea Peoples". *CAH* Vol. 2, Chap. 28.

- 1969a. "Ezekiel and Tyre". *Eretz -Israel* 9:6-13. Jerusalem.

- 1975. *A Catalogue of the Nimrud Ivories with other Examples of Ancient Near Eastern Ivories in the British Museum.* 2 ed. London.

- 1982. *Ancient Ivories in the Middle East and Adjacent Countries. Qedem* 14. Jerusalem.

- 1983. "Phoenician and Punic Art and Handicrafts. Some Reflections and Notes". *I Congresso Internazionale di Studi Fenici e Punici*:19-26.

Barnett, R.D. & Mendelson, C. 1987 (Eds.). *Tharros, a Catalogue of Material in the British Museum from Phoenician and Other Tombs at Tharros, Sardinia.* London.

Barrelet, M.T. 1952. "A propos d'une plaquette trouvée à Mari". *Syria* 29:285-293.

- 1955. "Les Déesses armies et ailées". *Syria* 32:233-260.

Bass, G.F. 1986. *"*A Ship at Ulu Burun (Kas):1984 Campaign". *AJA* 90:269-296.

Baumgarten, A.I. 1981. *The Phoenician History of Philo of Byblos: A Commentary.* Leiden.

Beazley, J.D. & Ashmole, B. 1971. *Greek Sculpture and Painting.* New York.

Beazley, J.D. 1939. "Excavations at Al Mina. Sueidia III. The Red-Figured Vases". *JHS* 59:1-44.

- 1944. "Groups of Early Attic Black-Figure". *Hesperia* 13:38-83.

- 1946. *Potters and Painter in Ancient Athens.* London.

- 1952. *The Development of Attic Black-Figure.* Berkeley.

- 1963. *Attic Red-Figure Vase-Painters.* Oxford.

Benson, J.L. 1953. *Die Geschichte der korinthischen Vasen.* Basel

- 1971. *The Oberdan Workshop. AJA* 75:83-85

- 1989. *Corinthian Workshop, Scripta Minora* I. Amsterdam.

- 1995. "Human Figures and Narrative in the Later Protocorinthian Vase Painting". *Hesperia* 64:163-177.

- 1995a. "Human Figures, The Ajax Painter and Narrative Scenes in Earlier Corinthian Vase Painting". In: Eds. J.C. Carter & S. Morris: *The Ages of Homer.* Austin-Texas.

Benz, F.L. 1972. *Personal Names in the Phoenician and Punic Inscriptions.* Rome.

Bérard, V.1902-3. *Les Phéniciens et l'Odysée.* 2 Vols. Paris.

Bernal, M. 1991. *Black Athena. The Afroasiatic Roots of Classical Civilization.* London.

Bietak, M. 1981. *Avaris and Piramesse: Archaeological Excavation in the Eastern Nile Delta.* Oxford.

Biers, W.R. & Gerhadt. K. O. & Braniff. R. A. 1995. "Scientific investigations of Corinthian 'plastic' vase" *AJA* 99 (2):320.

Bikai, P.M. 1978. *The Pottery of Tyre.* Warminster.

- 1978a. "The Late Phoenician Pottery Complex and Chronology". *BASOR* 229:47-55.

- 1981. *The Phoenician Imports.* In: Ed. V. Karageorghis. *Excavation at Kition* IV, *The Non-Cypriote Pottery.* Nicosia.

- 1987. *The Phoenician Pottery of Cyprus.* Nicosia

- 1990. Suggested Reading. *The Phoenicians: A Bibliography. BASOR* 279:65-66.

- 1992. "Cyprus and Phoenicia: Literary Evidence for the Early Iron Age". In: Ed. G.C. Ioannides, *Studies in Honour of Vassos Karageorghis*:241-248. Nicosia.

Billigmeier, J.C. 1982. *Kadmos and the Possibility of a West Semitic Presence in Helladic Greece.* Berkely.

Bisi, M. 1965. *Il Grifone.* Roma.

Blome, P. 1982. *Die Figürliche Bildwelt Kretas in der geometrischen und fruharchaischen Epoche.* Mainz.

- 1985. "Phönizische Dämonen auf einem attischen Krater". *Archäologischer Anzeiger* 573-579.

- 1990. (Ed.) *Orient und Frühes Griechenland. Kunstwerke der Sammlung H. und T. Bosshard.* Basel.

Boardman, J. 1959. "Greek Potters at Al Mina?" *Anatolian Studies* 9:161-169.

- 1961. *The Cretan Collection in Oxford. The Dictaean Cave and Iron Age Crete.* Oxford.

- 1965. "Tarsus, Al Mina and Greek Chronology". *JHS* 85:5-15.

- 1968. *Archaic Greek Gems.* London.

- 1970. "Orientalen auf Kreta". In: *Dädalische Kunst auf Kreta im 7. Jh. v. Chr.* Hamburg.

- 1974. *Athenian Black figure Vases.* London.

- 1975. *Athenian Red Figure Vases. The Archaic Period.* London.

- 1975a. *Greek Art.* London.

- 1985. *The Greeks Overseas.* London.

- 1987. "Amasis: The Implications of his name" in: Ed. M. True, *Papers on the Amasis and his World.* Malibu:141-152.

- 1990. "Al Mina and History". *Oxford Journal of Archaeology* 9:169- 90.

- 1996. *Greek Sculpture. The Archaic Period.* London.

- 2001. *Greek Gems and Finger Rings. Early Bronze Age to Late Classical.* London.

- 2001a. *The History of Greek Vases.* London.

Bonnet, C. 1988. *Melquart: Cultes et Mythes de l'Héraclés Tyrien en Mediterranée. Studia Phoenicia* 8.

Borell, B. 1978. *Attisch-geometrische Schalen. Eine Spätgeometrische Keramikgattung und ihre Beziehungen zum Orient*. Mainz.

Braun, T.F.R.G. 1982. "The Greeks in the Near East". *CAH* III:1-31

1982a. "The Greeks in Egypt". *CAH* III:32-56.

Brown, P. 1969. *The Lebanon and Phoenicia. Ancient Text Illustrating their Physical Geography and Native Industries. Vol. I, The Physical Setting and the Forest*. Beirut 1969.

Brown, R.B. 1975. *A Provisional Catalogue of and Commentary on Egyptain and Egyptianizing Artifacts found on Greek Sites*. Crookston, Minn'.

Bunimovitz, S.1987. "Minoan-Mycenaean olive oil production and trade- a review of current research" in: Eds. M. Heltzer & D. Eitam, *Olive Oil in Antiquity: Israel and Neighboring Countries from the Neolithic to the Early Arab Period*. Haifa.

Bunnens, G. 1979. *L'expansion Phénicienne en Méditerranée. In*: Ed. T.E. Levy, *The Archaeology of Society in the Holy Land*. Chap. 19:320-331. Brussels-Rome.

Burkert, W. 1975. "Rešep-Figuren, Apollon von Amyklai und die 'Erfindung' des Opfers auf Cypern". *Grazer Beiträge* 4:51-79.

- 1979. *Structure and History in Greek Mythology and Ritual*. Berkeley.

- 1984. *Die orietalisierende Epoche in der griechischen Religion und Literatur*. Heidelberg.

- 1985. *Greek Religion. Archaic and Classical*. Oxford & Cambridge, Mass.

- 1987. *Ancient Mystery Cults*. Cambridge, Mass.

- 1987a. "Oriental and Greek Mythology: The Meeting of Parallels". In: Ed. J. Bremmer, *Interpretations of Greek Mythology*:10-40. London.

- 1991. "Hommerstudien und Orient". In: Ed. Latacz, J. *Zweihundert Jahre Homer-forschung*:155-181. Stuttgart

- 1992. *The Orientalizing Revolution. Near Eastern Influence on Greek Culture in the Early Archaic Age*. London.

Burstein, S.M. 1996. "Greek Contact with Egypt and the Levant: Ca. 600-500 B.C. An Overview". In: *Coins, Cults, History and Inscriptions* III. *Studies in Honor of Al. N. Oikonomides. The Ancient World*:Vol. XXVII, 1. Chicago.

Callipolitis-Feytmans, D.1970. "Démeter, Corè et les Moires sur des Vases Corinthiens". *BCH* 94:45-65.

Cameron, M.A.S. 1970. "New Restorations of Minoan Frescos from Knosos". *Bulletin of the Institute of Classical Studies* 17:163-6.

Camp, J. 1986. *The Athenian Agora*. London.

Canby, J.V. 1975. "The Walters Gallery Cappadocian Tablet and the Sphinx in Anatolia in the Second Millennium B.C". *JNES* 34:225-248.

Canciani, F. 1970. *Bronze orientali e orientalizzanti a Creta nell' VIII e VII sec. A.C.* Rome.

Carpenter, R. 1958. "Phoenicians in the West". *AJA* 62:35-53.

Carter, J.B. 1985. *Greek Ivory-Carving in the Orientalizing and Archaic Period.* New York.

- 1987. "The Masks of Ortheia" *AJA 91:355-383.*

Casson, L. 1971. *Ships and Seamanship in the Ancient World*. Princeton.

Catalogue 1986. *Les Pheniciens et Le Monde Mediterraneen*. Bruxelles.

Charbonneaux, J. & Martin, R. & Villard, F. 1971. *Archaic Greek Art*. London-New York.

Chavalas, M.W. 1992. "Ancient Syria: A Historical Sketch". In: *New Horizons in The Study of Ancient Syria. Bibliotheca Mesopotamica*. 5: 1-21.

Chehab, M. 1983. "Découvertes phéniciennes au Liban". *I Congresso Internazionale di Studi Fenici e Punici* (1979):165-172. Roma.

Ciasca, A. 1982. "Insediamenti e cultura dei Fenici a Malta". In: Ed. H.G. Niemeyer, *Die Phönizier im Westen*:133-151. Mainz.

- 1994. *Scavi a Mozia: Le Terrecotte Figurate*. Roma.

Clifford, R.J. 1990. "Phoenician Religion". *BASOR* 279:55-65.

Coldstream, J.N. 1968. *Greek Geometric Pottery*. London.

- 1969. "The Phoenicians of Ialysos". *BICS* 16:1-8.

Coldstream, J.N. and G.L. Huxley. 1972. *Kythera*. London.

- 1977. *Geometric Greece*. London.

- 1978. *Deities in Aegean Art*. Inaugural Lecture. London.

- 1982. "Greeks and Phoenicians in the Aegean". In: Ed. H.G. Niemeyer, *Die Phönizier im Westen* (1982):261-272.

Coldstream, J.N. & Bikai, P.M. 1988. "Early Greek Pottery in Tyre and Cyprus: Some Preliminary Comparisons". *Report of the Department of Antiquities*: part 2:35-44. Cyprus.

- 1990. "Greek Temples: Why and where?". In: Eds. P.E. Easterling, & J.V. Muir, *Greek Religion and Society*:68-79. Cambridge.

Coleman, J.E. & Walz, C.A (Eds.) 1997. *Greeks and Barbarians*. Bethseda, MD.

Cook, B.F. 1972. "A Protocorinthian Aryballos and Three Late Corinthian Vases". *BMQ* 36:3-4,110-117, Pls. 38-9.

Cook, J.M. 1947. "Attic Workshops Around 700 B.C.". In: *Annual of the British School at Athens* 42.

- 1962. *The Greeks in Ionia and the East*. London.

Cook, R.M. 1967. "Origins of Greek Sculpture". *JHS* 87:24-31.

- 1997. *Greek Painted Pottery.* London & New York.

Coulsen, W.D.E. 1990. *The Greek Dark Ages.* Athens.

Coulton, J.J. 1977. *Ancient Greek Architects at Work.* London.

Corbett, J.H. 1982. "Thither came Phoenicians": The Greeks and the Phoenicians from Homer to Alexander". *Scripta Mediterranea,* III:72-92.

Courbin, P. 1986. "Bassit". *Syria* 63:175-219.

- 1990. "Bassit-Posidaion in the Early Iron Age". In: Ed. J.P. Descouedres, *Greek Colonists and Native Populations.* Proceedings of the First Australian Congress of Classical Archaeology held in Honour of Emeritus Prof. A.D. Trendall (Sydney):503-9. Canberra.

- 1993. "Fragments d'amphores protogéométriques á Bassit". *Hesperia* 62:95-113.

Crowley, J.L. 1989. *The Aegean and The East. Transference of Artistic Motifs (between the Aegean, Egypt and the Near East in the Bronze Age).* Jansered.

Crielaard, J.P. 1991-1992. "How the West was won: Euboeans vs. Phoenicians". *Hamburger Beiträge zur Archäology:18-19,235-249.*

Culican, W. - 1970. "Phoenician Oil Bottles and Tripod Bowls". *Berytus* XIX: 5-16.

- 1970a. "Almuñecar, Assur and Phoenician Penetration of the Western Mediterranean". *Levant* 2:28-36.

- 1973. "Phoenician Jewellery in New York and Copenhagen". *Berytus* XXII:31-52.

- 1975-6. "Some Phoenician Masks and Terracottas. *Berytus* XXIV:47-87.

- 1982. "The Repertoire of Phoenician pottery". In: Ed. H.G. Niemeyer, *Phönizier im Westen:45-82.*

Curtis, J. 1988. (Ed.) *Bronzeworking Centres of Western Asia c. 1000- 539 B.C.* London.

Dawkins, R. 1929. *The Sanctuary of Arthemis Orthia at Sparta.* London.

Demargne, P. 1964. *The Birth of Greek Art.* Golden Press. New York.

Dessene, A. 1957. "Le Griffon Créto-mycénien". *BCH* 81:203-11.

- 1957 *Le Sphinx. Étude iconographique.* Écoles Francaises d'Athenes et de Rome.

De Vries, K. 1977. "Attic Pottery in the Achaemenid Empire". *AJA* 81:544-548.

Drews, R. 1979. "Phoenician, Carthage and the Spartan Eunomia". *American Journal of Philology* 100:45-58.

Du Plat Taylor, J. 1959. "The Cypriot and Syrian Pottery from Al Mina, Syria". *Iraq* 21:62-69.

Dunbabin, T.J. 1948. *The Western Greeks.* Oxford.

- & Robertson, M. 1953. "Some Protocorinthian Vase-painters". In: *Annual of the British School at Athens* 48. London

- 1962. *Perachora* II, Oxford.

- 1979. *The Greeks and their Eastern Neighbours. Studies in the Relations between Greece and the Countries of the Near East in the 8th and 7th Centuries B.C. JHS* Suppl. 8. London.

Dussaud, R. 1946-8. "Melqart", *Syria* XXV (1946-1948):205-230.

Cyprus 1996. *Cyprus Heritage. The Art of Ancient Cyprus as Exhibited at the Cyprus Museum* (Text: Pavlos Flourentzos) Limassol.

Edwards, R.B. 1979. *Kadmos the Phoenician. A Study in Greek Legends and the Mycenaean Age.* Amsterdam.

Elayi, J. & Cavigneaux, A. 1979. "Sargon II et les Ioniens". *Oriens Antiquus* 18:59-75.

Farnell, L.R. 1896. *The Cults of the Greek States.* 5 Vols. Oxford.

Finley, M.I. 1970. *Early Greece.* London.

Fleming, W.B. 1966. *The History of Tyre.* New York.

Forbes, R.J. 1965. *Studies in Ancient Technology 3.* Leiden

Frankenstein, S. 1979. "The Phoenicians in the Far West: A Function of Neo-Assyrian Imperialism". In: Ed. M.T. Larsen, *Power and Propaganda:*263-294. Copenhagen.

Frankfort, H. 1936-7. "Notes on the Cretan Griffin". *Annual of the British School at Athens* 37:106-122.

Gehrig, U. und Niemeyer, H.G. (Eds.) 1990. *Die Phönizier im Zeitalter Homers.* (Texte & Katalog) Mainz.

Gjerstad, E. 1977. *Greek Geometric and Archaic Pottery found in Cyprus.* Stockholm.

Gonzales, P.V. 1996. *La Isla de Malta en Epoca Fenicia y Punica.* Oxford.

Graham, A.J. 1986. "The Historical Interpretation of Al Mina". *Dialogues d'Histoire Ancienne* 12:51-65.

Gubel, E. 1983. "Art in Tyre During the first and second Iron Age". *Studia Phoenicia* I:23-52. Leuven.

- 1985. "Phoenician Lioness Heads from Nimrud. Origin and Function". In: *Studia Phoenicia* III 185-202. Leuven.

- 1987. "'Syro-Cypriote' Cubical Stamps: The Phoenician Connection". In: Ed. E. Lipinski, *SPV:*195-224. Leuven.

- 1987. *Phoenician Furniture. Studia Phoenicia* VII. Leuven.

- 1990. "Die Phönizische Kunst". In: Eds. U. Gehrig, & G. Niemeyer, *Die Phönizier im Zeitalter Homers:*75-86. Mainz.

Gubel, E. & Lipinski, E. (Eds.) 1985. *Phoenicia and Its Neighbours. Studia Phoenicia* III. Leuven.

Guterbock, H.G. 1957. "Narration in Anatolian, Syrian and Assyrian Art". *AJA* 61:62-71.

Hachmann, R. 1983. (Ed.) *Frühe Phöniker im Lebanon: 20 Jahre deutsche Ausgrabungen in Kamid el-Loz.* Mainz am Rhein.

Hallett, C.H. 1986. "The Origins of the Classical Style in Sculpture". *JHS* 106:71-84.

Hampe, R., Simon, E. 1981. *The Birth of Greek Art from Mycenaean to the Archaic Period.* London.

Hanfmann, G.M.A. 1948. "Archaeology in Homeric Asia Minor". *AJA* 52:135-155.

Hanky, V. 1967. "Mycenaean Pottery in the Middle East: Notes and Finds Since 1951". *Annual of the British School at Athens* 62:107-148, Pls. 26-37.

Harden, D. 1948. "The Phonicians in the West Coast of Africa". *Antiquity* XXII 87:141-150.

- 1962 *The Phoenicians*. London.

Harlow, P.A. 1977. "Potnia-Theron: The Winged Artemis motif in Corinthian Vase-Painting". *M.A Thesis*. Berkely.

Hartog. F. 1988. *The Mirror of Herodotus: The Representation of the Other in the Writing of History*. Berkeley.

Hawkins, D. 1996 "The Hittites and their Empire". In: Ed. J.G. Westenholz, *Royal Cities of the Biblical World*. Jerusalem.

Helm, P.R. 1980. *'Greeks' in the Neo-Assyrian Levant and 'Assyria' in Early Greek Writers*. Philadelphia.

Herm, G. 1973. *Die Phoenizier. Das Purpurreich der Antik*. Düsseldorf.

Hermann, H.V. 1980. *Die Funde aus Olympia*. München

Higgins, R.A. 1967. *Greek Terracottas*. London.

- 1969. "Early Greek Jewellery". *BSA* 64:143-153.

- 1997. *Minoan and Mycenaean art*. London.

Hopkins, C. 1965. "Astrological Interpretations of Some Phoenician Bowls". *JNES* 24: 28-36.

Hopkins, K. & Whittaker, C.R. 1994. "The Growth and Standing of the Early Western colonies". In: Eds. G.R. Tsetskhladze & F. De Angelis, *Archaeology of the Greek Colonisation, Essays Dedicated to Sir John Boardman*, 40:1-10. Oxford.

Hopper, R.J. 1949. "Addenda to Necrocorinthia" *BSA* 44:162-257.

Hurwit, J. 1985. *The Art and Culture of Early Greece*, 1100-1480 B.C. Ithaca (N.Y).

Hunt, D. 1984. (Ed.) *Footprints in Cyprus. An Illustrated History*. London.

Iliffe, J.H. 1932. "Pre-Hellenistic Greek Pottery in Palestine". *QDAP* 2:15-26.

Imai, I. 1977. *Some Aspects of the Phoenician Bowls*. New York.

Immerwahr, S.A. 1971. *The Athenian Agora Vol. XIII: The Neolithic and Bronze Ages*. Princeton.

Jantzen, U. 1972. *Aegyptische and Orientalische Bronzen aus dem Hera*ion von *Samo*s. (Samos 8) Bonn.

Jeffery, L.H. 1976. *Archaic Greece. The City-States c. 700-500 B.C.* London & Tunbridge.

- 1990. *The Local Script of Archaic Greece. A Study of the Origins of the Greek Alphabet and its Development from the Eighth to the Fifth Centuries B.C.* Oxford.

Jenkins, I. 2002. "The Earliest Representations in Greek Art of the Death of Ajax". In: Ed. A. Pierson, *Essays in Honour of Dietrich von Bothmer*, 14:153-156. Amsterdam.

Jidejian, N. 1968. *Byblos through the Ages*. Beirut.

- 1969. *Tyre through the Ages*. Beirut.

- 1971. *Sidon through the Ages*. Beirut.

Johansen, F. 1923. *Les Vases Sicyoniens*. Copenhagen.

Johnstone, A. 1995. "Pre Classical Greece". In: Ed. J. Boardman, *Oxford History of Classical Art*. Oxford.

Johnstone, W. 1978. "Cursive Phoenician and the Archaic Greek Alphabet". *Kadmos* 17:151-166.

Jucker, I. 1963. "Frauenfest in Korinth". *Antike Kunst 6:47-61*.

Kantor, H. 1947. *The Aegean and the Orient in the Second Millennium B.C.* Bloomington, Ind.

Kantor, H.J. 1956. "Syro-Palestinian Ivories" *Journal of Near Eastern Studies* 15:153-174.

- 1958. "The Ivories from Floor 6 of Sounding IX". In: Ed. C. W. McEwan, et al. *Sounding at Tell Fakhariyah*:57-58. Chicago.

- 1960. "Ivory Carving in the Mycenaean Period". *Archaeology* 13:14-25

- 1962. "A Bronze Plaque with a Relief Decoration from Tell Tainat". *JNES* 21:93-117.

Karageorghis, V. 1976. *Kition: Mycenaean and Phoenician Discoveries in Cyprus*. London.

- 1979. (Ed.) The Relations between Cyprus and Crete, 2000-500 B.C. In: *Acts of the International Archaeological Symposium*. Nicosia.

- 1981. *Kition IV, The Non-Cypriote Pottery*. Nicosia.

- 1985. *Kition V, The Pre-Phoenician Levels*. Nicosia.

- 1986. (Ed.) *Cyprus between the Orient and the Occident*. Nicosia.

- 1997. "Greek Gods and Heroes in Cyprus: A preview of the Problem". In: Ed. O. Palagia, *Greek Offerings, Essays on Greek Art in Honour of John Boardman*. Monograph 89:221-229. Oxbow.

- 2001. "Why White Slip?" In: *The White Slip Ware of Late Bronze Age Cyprus*. Proceeding of an International Conference, (Nicosia):6-13. Wien.

Katzenstein, H.J. 1973. *The History of Tyre* (Revised Edition). Be'er Sheva.

Kaulen, G. 1967. *Werkstätten griechischer Kleinplastik des 7. Jh. v. Chr.* Munich.

Kearsley, R. 1989. *The Pendent Semi-Circle Skyphos: A Study of its Development and Chronology and an Examination of it as Evidence for Euboean Activity at Al Mina*. London.

Knapp, A.B. 1985. "Alashiya, Caphtor/Keftiu and Eastern Mediterranean Trade". *Journal of Field Archaeology* 12:231-250.

- 1991. "Spice, drugs, grain and grog: organic goods in Bronze Age east Mediterranean trade" in: Ed. N.H. Gale, *Bronze Age Trade in the Mediterranean. Studies in Mediterranean Archaeology 90*. Göteborg.

Knapp, A.B. et al. 1994. *Proveniennce Studies and Bronze Age Cyprus: Production Exchange and Politico-Economic Change.* Madison (Wisconsin).

Kochavi, M. 1990. "Some Connections between the Aegean and the Levant in the Second Millennium B.C., A View from the East". In: Eds. G. Kocke & I. Tokumaru, *Greece Between East and West: 10th-8th Centuries B.C.* Mainz.

Kopcke, G. & Tokumaru, I. (Eds.) 1990. *Greece between East and West.* Papers of the Meeting at the Institute of fine Arts, N.Y. Uni., March 15-16th, 1990. Mainz.

Korres, G. 1988. (Ed.) *The Prehistoric Aegean and its Relation to Adjacent Areas.* Athens.

Korti-Konti, S. 1997. "The Orientalising Period in Macedonia". In: Ed. O. Palagia, *Greek Offerings.* Essays on Greek Art in Honour of John Boardman Monograph 89:55-62. Oxbow.

Kraiker, W. 1951. *Aegina.* Berlin.

Kübler, K. 1959, 1970. *Kerameikos: Ergebnisse der Ausgrabungen,* VI:1and 2: *Die Nekropole des späten 8. bis frühen 6. Jahrhunderts.* Berlin.

Kunze, E. 1931. *Kretische Bronzereliefs.* Stuttgart.

Kyrieleis, H. 1979. "Babylonische Bronzen im Heraion von Samos". *Jahrbuch des Deutschen Archäologischen Instituts* 94:32-48. Athen.

Labat, R. 1967. "Assyrien und seine Nachbarländer (Babylonien, Elam, Ionien). Von 1000-617 v. Chr. Das neubabylonische Reich bis 539 v. Chr". In: Fischer Weltgeschichte. Vol. IV: *Die altorientalischen Reiche* III:9-111. Frankfurt.

Labib, B. 1981. *Phoenician Sport. Its Influence on the Origin of the Olympic Games.* Amsterdam.

Lamb, W.H 1929. *Greek and Roman Bronzes.* London.

Liebowitz, H. 1987. "Late Bronze II Ivory Work in Palestine. Evidence of a Cultural High Point". *BASOR 265: 3-24.*

Lipinsky, E. 1986. "Zeus Ammon et Baal Hammon? A propos d'Un Bronze de Genoni (Sardaigne)". *Studia Phoenicia* IV:307-322.

- 1987. (Ed.) *Phoenicia and the East Mediterranean in the First Millennium B.C. Studia Phoenicia* V. Leuven.

- 1988. "Les Phéniciens et L'alphbet". *Oriens Antiquus* 27:231-260.

Lo Porto, F.G. 1959/60. "Ceramica arcaica della necropolis di Taranto". *Annuario Scuola di Atene* 37/8. N.S 21/2:1-230.

Maass, E. 1903. *Griechen und Semiten auf dem Isthmus von Korinth.* Berlin.

Manchester, K.L. 1991. *The Protocorinthian Black-Polychrome Technique.* Los Angeles.

Markoe, G. 1985. *Phoenician Bronze and Silver Bowls from Cyprus and the Mediterranean. Uni. of California Classical Studies* 26. Berkeley.

- 1990. "The Emergence of Phoenician Art". *BASOR* 279:13-27.

- 1996. "The Emergence of Orientalizing in Greek Art: Some Observations on the Interchange between Greeks and Phoenicians in the 8th and 7th Cents. BC". *BASOR* 301:47-67.

- 2000. *Phoenicians.* Berkeley. L.A.

- 2003. "Phoenician Metal Work Abroad: a Question of Export or On-Site Production?" In: Eds. V. Karageorghis & N. Stambolidis, *Sea Routes... Interconnections in the Mediterranean 16th-6th c. BC.* Athens.

Massa, A. 1977. *The Phoenicians.* Geneve.

Michaelidou-Nicolaou, I. 1987. "Repercussions of the Phoenician Presence in Cyprus". In: *SPV* (Ed. E. Lipinski): 331-338.

Morris, I 1987. *Burial and Ancient Society: the Rise of the Greek City State.* Cambridge.

Morris, S. 1984. *The Black and White Style: Athens and Aigina in the Orientalizing Period.* Yale Classical Monographs 6. New Haven.

- 1989. "Daidalos and Kadmos: Classicism and 'Orientalism'". *Arethusa* 22:39-51.

- 1990. "Greece and the Levant". In: *Discussion and Debate: Special Review Section on M. Bernal: Black Athena: The Afroasiatic Roots of Classical Civilization,* Vol. I: *The Fabrication of Ancient Greece. Journal of Mediterranean Archaeology* 3/1:57-66.

- 1995. *Daidalos and the Origins of Greek Art.* Princeton.

Morris, S. & Papadopoulos, J.K. 1998. "Phoenicians and the Corinthian Pottery Industry" in: Eds. R. Rolle, K. Schmidt & R.F. Docter, *Archaologische Studien Kontaktzonen der antiken Welt*:251-263.Gottingen.

Moscati, S. 1960. *Ancient Semitic Civilizations.* New York.

- 1968. *The World of the Phoenicians. History of Civilization.* London

- 1982. "L'espansione fenicia nel Mediterraneo Occidentale". In: Ed. H.G. Niemeyer, *Phönizier im Westen*:5-11. Mainz.

- 1983. "Precolonizzazione greca e precolonizzazione fenicia". *Rivista di Studi Fenici* XI:169-187.

- 1986. *Italia Punica.* Milan.

- 1988. (Ed.) *The Phoenicians.* Catalogue. Comitato Amici di Palazzo Grassi. Venezia.

- 1990. *L'arte dei Fenici.* Milan.

Muhly, J. 1970. "Homer and the Phoenicians: The Relations between Greece and the Near East in the Late Bronze and Early Iron Age". *Berytus* 19:19-64.

Murray, O. 1993. *Early Greece.* 2nd ed. London.

Nagy, G. 1979. *The Best of Achaeans: Concepts of the Hero in Archaic Greek Art and Poetry*. Baltimore.

Neeft, C.W. 1987. *Protocorinthian Subgeometric Aryballoi*. Amsterdam.

Negbi, O. *1979. Cannanite Gods in Metal: An Archaeological Study of Ancient Syro-Palestinian Figurines*. Tel Aviv.

- 1982. "Evidence for Early Phoenician Communities in the East Mediterranean Islands". *Levant* 14:179-82.

- 1988. "Levantine Elements in the Sacred Architecture of the Aegean". *Annual of the British School at Athens* 83:339-357.

- 1992. "Early Phoenician Presence in the Mediterranean Islands: A Repraisal". *AJA* 96:4, 599-615.

Niemeyer, H.G. 1982. (Ed.) *Phönizier im Westen*. Mainz.

1984. "Die Phönizier und die Mittelmeerwelt im Zeitalter Homers". *Jahrbuch des Römisch-Germanischen Zentralmuseums* 31:1-94. Mainz.

- 1989. *Das Frühe Kartago und die Phönizische Expansion im Mittelmeerraum*. Göttingen.

- 1990. "The Phoenicians in the Mediterranean: A Non-Greek Model for Expansion and Settlement in Antiquity". In: Ed. J.P. Descoeudres, *Greek Colonists and Native Popul*ations:469-489. Oxford.

- 1990a. *Greek Colonists and Native Populations*: Proceedings of the First Australian Congress of Classical Archaeology held in Honour of Emeritus Professor A.D. Trendall. Oxford.

- 1993. "Trade Before the Flag? On the Principles of Phoenician Expansion in the Mediterranean". *Biblical Archaeology Today*, 1990. Proceedings of the Second International Congress on Biblical Archaeology. Israel Exploration Society 1993:335-343. Jerusalem.

- 2003. "On Phoenician Art and its Role in Trans-Mediterranean Interconnections ca.1100-600 BC". In: Eds. V. Karageorghis, & N. Stambolidis, *Sea Routes... Interconnections in the Mediterranean 16th-6th BC*. Athens.

Palagia, O. 1997. "Reflections on the Piraeus Bronzes". In: Ed. O. Palagia, *Greek Offerings, Essays on Greek Art in Honour of John Boardman* Monograph 89:177-195. Oxbow.

Parrot, A., Chehab, M. et Moscati, S. 1975. *Les Phenicie*ns. *L'expansion Phenicienne*. Paris.

Payne, H. 1931. *Necrocorinthia*. Oxford.

- 1933. *Protokorinthische Vasenmalerei. Bildergriechischer Vasen, Heft 7.*

Peckham, B.1987".Phoenicia and the Religion of Israel: the Epigraphic Evidence". In: Eds. P.H. Miller, et al. *Ancient Israelite Religion: Essays in Honor of Frank Moore Cross*:79-99. Philadelphia.

Pemberton, E. 1989. Sanctuary of Demeter and Kore - he Greek Pottery. *Corinth*, Vol. XVIII. Athens.

Perkins, A. 1957. "Narration in Babylonian Art". *AJA* 61:54-62.

Perrot, G.& Chipiez, Ch. 1885 *History of Art in Phoenicia and its Dependencies*. London.

Picard, G.C. & Picard, C. 1969. *The life and Death of Carthage*. New York.

Pollitt, J.J. 1974. *The Ancient View of Greek Art: Criticism, History, and Terminology*. New Haven.

- 1987. "Pots, Politics and Personifications in Early Classical Athens". *Yale Uni. Art Gallery Bulletin*:11-12.

Popham, M.R., Sackett, L.H, & Themelis, P.G. 1980. *Lefkandi. The Iron Age*. Vol. 1: *The C*emeteries. *BSA* Suppl. 11. London.

- Touloupa, E. & Sackett, L.H. 1982. "Further Excavations of the Toumba Cemetery at Lefkandy, 1981.*BSA* 77:213-248.

- 1994. "Precolonisation: Early Greek Contact with the East". In: Eds. G.R. Tsetskhladze & F. De Angelis, *The Archaeology of Greek Colonisation*. Oxford Uni. Committee for Archaeology, Monograph 40:11-34. Oxford.

Poulsen, F. 1912. *Der Orient und die frühgriechische Kunst*. Leipzig.

Powell, B.B. 1991. *Homer and the Origin of the Alphabet*. Cambridge.

Pritchard, J.B. 1978. *Recovering Sarepta, A Phoenician City*. Princeton.

- 1988. *Sarepta IV (The Objects from Area II,X)*. Lebanon.

Raban, A. (Ed.) 1985. *Harbour Archaeology*. Oxford.

- 1997. "Phoenician Harbours in the Levant". *Michmanim* 11:7-27.

Rasmussen, T. 1991. "Corinth and the Orientalizing Phenomenon". In: Eds. T. Rasmussen, & N. Spivey, *Looking at Greek Vases*:57-78. Cambridge.

Richter, G.M.A. 1949. *Archaic Greek Art*. Oxford.

- 1961. *The Archaic Gravestones of Attica*. London.

- 1968. *Korai: Archaic Greek Maidens. A Study of the Development of the Kore Type in Greek Sculpture*. New York.

- 1970. *Kouroi: A Study of the Greek Kouros Type from the Late Seventh to the Early Fifth Century B.C.* New York.

- 1974. *Greek Art*. London.

Ridgway, B. 1977. *The Archaic Style in Greek Sculpture*. Princeton.

Ridgway, D. and Ridgway, F.R. 1979 *Italy before the Romans. The Iron Age, Orientalising and Etruscan Periods*. London.

Ridgway, D. 1992. *The First Western Greeks*. Cambridge.

- 1992. "Damaratus and predecessors". In: Eds. G. Kopcke, & I. Tokumaru, *Greece Between East and West 10th-8th Centuries BC*. Mainz.

- 1994. "Phoenicians and Greeks in the West: A View from Pithekoussai". In: Eds. G.R. Tsetskhlade, & F. de Angelis. *The Archaeology of Greek Colonisation*. Oxford Uni. Committee for Archaeology Monograph 40:35-46. Oxford.

Riis, P.J. 1970. *Sukas*. Vol. 1. Copenhagen.

- 1982. "Griechen in Phönizien". In: Ed. H.G. Niemeyer, *Phönizier im Westen*:237-255. Mainz.

Ritting, D. 1977. *Assyrisch-Babylonische Kleinplastik magischer Bedeutung vom 13.-6. Jh. v. Chr*. Munich.

Rizza, G. & Santa Maria Scrinari, V. 1968. *Il santuario sull'acropoli di Gortina*. Vol. 1. Rome.

Robertson, M. 1977. *A History of Greek Art*. 2 Vols. Cambridge.

Röllig, W. 1982. "Die Phönizier des Mutterlands zur Zeit der Kolonisation". In: Ed. H.G. Niemeyer, *Phönizier im Westen*:15-28.Mainz.

- 1983. "On the Origin of the Phoenicians". *Berytus* XXXI:79-93.

Sakellarakis, Y.A. 1993. "Ivory Trade in the Aegean in the 8th Century B.C.E". In: *2nd. International Congress of Biblical Archaeology, Jerusalem* 1990:345-366. Jerusalem.

Salmon, J.B. 1984. *Wealthy Corinth. A History of the City to 338 B.C*. Oxford.

Sandars, N.K. 1978. *The Sea Peoples*. London.

Schaeffer.C.F.A 1939-1940 *Ugaritica I, II*. Paris.

Schefold, K. 1966. *Myth and Legend in Early Greek Art*. New York.

- 1967. *Die Griechen und ihre Nachbarn* (Propyläen Kunstgeschichte. 1) Berlin.

Seibert, I. 1974. *Woman in Ancient Near East*. Leipzig.

Schepens, G. 1987. "The Phoenicians in Ephorus Universal History". *SPV* 315-330.

Schweitzer, B. 1918. *Untersuchungen zur Chronologie dergeometrische Stillein Griechenland*. Heidelberg.

Shanks, M. 1999. *Art and the Greek State*. Cambridge.

Shaw, J.W. 1989. "Phoenicians in Southern Crete". *AJA* 93:165-183.

Shelmerdine, C.W. 1985. *The perfume industry of Mycenaean Pylos*. Göteborg.

Sherratt, S & A. 1993. "The Growth of the Mediterranean Economy in the Early First Millennium B.C" in: *Ancient Trade: New Perspective. World Archaeology:* Vol. 24, No. 3:361-378.

Snodgrass, A.M. 1972. *The Dark Age of Greece*. Edinburgh.

- 1980. *Archaic Greece: the Age of Experiment*. London.

- 1983. "Heavy Freight in Archaic Greece". In: Eds. P. Garnsey., K. Hopkins & C.R. Whittacker, *Trade in the Ancient Economy*:16-26. London.

Stampolidis, N. 2002. "From the Geometric and Archaic Necropolis at Eleutherna". In: Eds. M. Stamatopoulou & M. Yeroulanou, *Excavating Classical Culture. Recent Archaeological Discoveries*, 327-332. Oxford.

- 2003 "On the Phoenician Presence in the Aegean" in: Eds. N.C. Stampolidis & V. Karageorghis, *Sea Routes... Interconnections in the Mediterranean*:217-232. Athens.

Steiner, A. 1992. "Pottery and Cult in Corinth, Oil and Water at the Sacred Spring". *Hesperia* 61:385-408.

Stern, E. 1990. "New Evidence from Dor for the First Appearance of the Phoenicians along the Northern Coast of Israel". *BASOR* 279:27-35.

Stern, E., Berg, J. & Sharon, I. 1991. "Tel Dor, 1988-1989: preliminary Report". *IEJ* 41:46-61.

- 1993. "The Many Masters of Dor. Part 2: How Bad Was Ahab?" *Biblical Archaeology Review* 19.2:18-36.

- 1994. "A Phoenician-Cypriote Votive Scapula from Tel Dor: A Maritime Scene". *IEJ* 44:1-2, 1-12.

Stieglitz, R.S. 1990. "The Geopolitics of Phoenician Littoral in the Early Iron Age". *BASOR* 279: 9-13.

Stillwell, A. & Benson, J.L.1984. *Corinth XV: 3, The Potters' Quarter: The Pottery*. Princeton.

Stoops, M.W. 1977-8. *Corinth VII:2 (*Review of Amyx, D.A. & Lawrence, P.). In: *BABesch* 52-3, 288.

Tamvaki, A. 1974. "The Seals and Sealings from the Citadel House Area: A Study in Mycenaean Glyptic and Iconography". *Annual of the British School at Athens* 69:259-294.

Tatton-Brown, V. 1989. (Ed.) *Cyprus and the Eastern Mediterranean in the Iron Age*. London.

Tsetskhladze, R.G. and De Angelis, F. 1994. (Eds.) *The Archaeology of Greek Colonisation. Essays Dedicated to Sir John Boardman*. Oxford Uni. Committee for Archaeology, Monograph 40. Oxford.

Villard, F. 1948. "La Chronologie de la céramique protocorinthienne". In: *Mélanges d'archéologie et d'historie*, 1-34.

Von Soden, W. 1994. *The Ancient Orient*. Grand Rapids.

Waldbaum, C. 1994. "Early Greek Contacts with the Southern Levant, ca. 1000-600 B.C.: The Eastern Perspective". *BASOR*:293, 53-66.

Ward, W.A. 1968. *The Role of the Phoenicians in the Interaction of Mediterranean Civilizations*. Beirut.

Ward, W.A. & Joukowsky, M.S. 1992. (Eds.). *The Crisis Years: The twelfth century B.C. from beyond the Danube to the Tigris*. Dunbuque.

Weinberg, S. 1941 "What is Protocorinthian Geometric Ware" *AJA 45:35-44*.

- 1943. *Corinth VII:1 The Geometric and Orientalizing Pottery*. Princeton.

- 1948. "A Cross-Section of Corinthian Antiquities (Excavations of 1940), *Hesperia* 17:190-241.

- 1949. "Investigations at Corinth, 1947-8". *Hesperia 18:148-157*.

Weinberg, S. et Weinberg, G. 1956. "Arachne of Lydia at Corinth". In: Ed. S. Weinberg, *The Aegean and the Near East: Studies Presented to Hetty Goldman*. Locust Valley, N.Y.

- 1963. Review of Dunbabin, T.J. et al. *Perachora* II (Oxford) in: *AJA* 67:425-426.

Wenning, R. 1989. "Mesad Hašavyahu. Ein Stutzpunkt des Jojakim?" in: Ed. F.L. Hossfeld, *Vom Sinai zum Horeb. Stationen altestamentlicher Glaubensgeschichte* 169-196. Würzburg.

- 1991. "Nachrichten über Griechen in Palästina in der Eisenzeit". In: Ed. J.M. Fossey, *Proceeding of the First International Congress on the Hellenic Diaspora from Antiquity to Modern Times*. Vol. 1:207-219. McGill Uni. Monographs in Classical Archaeology and History. Amsterdam.

West, M.L. 1999. *The East Face of Helicon: West Asiatic Elements in Greek Poetry and Myth*. Oxford.

Whitley, J. 2001. *The Archaeology of Ancient Greece*. Cambridge World Archaeology. Cambridge.

Williams, C.K. 1986. "Corinth and the cult of Aphrodite". In: Eds. M.A. Del Chairo, & W.R. Biers, *Corinthiaca: Studies in Honour of Darell A. Amyx*. Columbia (Missouri).

Williams, D. 2002. "Perfume Pots, Painters, and a Puzzling Pursuit". In: Ed. A. Pierson, *Essays in Honor of Dietrich von Bothmer, Text*, Vol. 14:341-8. Amsterdam.

Winter, I. 1979. *North Syria in the Early First Millennium B.C. with Special Reference to Ivory Carving*. Ph. D. diss. Columbia Uni. (1973). Ann Arbor (Michigan).

- 1995. "Homer's Phoenicians: History, Ethnography or Literary Trope?". In: Eds. J. Carter & S. Morris, *The Ages of Homer*: 247-271. Austin, Texas.

Yon, M. 1986. "Cultes Phéniciens à Chypre: Interprétation Chypriote". *Studia Phoenicia* IV:127-152.

- 1997. s.v. Ugarit. In: Ed. E.M. Meyers, *The Oxford Encyclopedia of Archaeology in the Near East, 5:255-262*. New York-Oxford.

- 2001. "White Slip Ware in the Northern Levant". In: Ed. V. Karageorghis, *The White Slip Ware of Late Bronze Age Cyprus:*117-125. Wien.

Zaccagnini, C. 1983. "Pattern of Mobility among Ancient Near Eastern Craftsmen". *JNES* 42:245-64.

SUGGESTED FURTHER READINGS

Betancourt, P.P. 2007. *Introduction to Aegean art*. Philadelphia: INSTAP Academic Press.

Hemingway, C. & Hemingway S. 2007. "Ancient Greek Colonization and Trade and their Influence on Greek Art". In: *Heilbrunn Timeline of Art History*. New York: The Metropolitan museum of Art, 2000–.

Kefalidou, E., 2001. "Polychrome Pottery from Aiani". *Hesperia* 70:189-219.

Langdon, S. 2008. *Art and identity in Dark Age Greece, 1100-700 B.C.E.* New York: Cambridge University

Moore, M.B. 2007. "The Princeton Painter in New York." *Metropolitan Museum Journal*, Vol. 42.

- 2000. "Ships on a 'Wine-Dark Sea' in the Age of Homer." *Metropolitan Museum Journal*, Vol. 35.

Norskov, V. 2002 . *Greek Vases in New Contexts, the collecting and trading of Greek vases – an aspect of the modern reception of antiquity*. Aarhus.

Pedley, J, G. 2005. *Sanctuaries and the Sacred in the Ancient Greek World*. Cambridge.

- 2007. *Greek art and Archaeology*. 4th ed. Upper Saddle River: Pearson Education.

Sowder, A. 2008. "Ancient Greek Bronze Vessels". In: *Heilbrunn Timeline of Art History*. New York: The Metropolitan Museum of Art, 2000–.

Strafford, E. J. 2004. *Life, Myth and Art in Ancient Greece*. Los Angeles: J. Paul Getty Museum,

Tsingarida, A. (ed.) 2009. *Shapes and Uses of Greek Vases*. Brussels.

Plate 13:2	Sphinx from the Artemision in Ephesus, made of ivory, end of the 7th century BC (H-S, 352).
Plate 13:3	Dress brooch ivory plate from the Artemis Orthia at Sparta, mid 7th century BC (H-S, 354).
Plate 13:4	Protoma of Artemis of Orthia from her temple in Sparta, around 600 BC (H-S, 355).
Plate 14:1-3	Head of Apollo Amiklaios, protoma (11.5 cm height) made of terracotta, from his temple in Sparta, around 700 BC (H-S, 397-399).
Plate 14:4	Gold sphinx from Perachora near Corinth, last quarter of the 7th century BC (H-S, 411).
Plate 15:1	Cylindrical seal from Syria, 1300-1200 BC (Cr, 120).
Plate 15:2	Cylindrical seal from Cyprus, 1500-1300 BC (Cr, 121B).
Plate 15:3	Mitanic cylindrical seal, 1500-1400 BC (Cr, 121A).
Plate 15:4	Fragment of fresco from Knossos, around 1500 BC (Cr, 113).
Plate 15:5	Segment of miniature fresco from Thera, around 1500 BC (Cr, 115).
Plate 15:6	A rectangular seal from Rutsi, around 1500 BC (Cr, 115).
Plate 15:7	Piece of gold jewelry from Mycenae, around 1500 BC (Cr, 116).
Plate 16:1	Proto-Attic pottery jar, around 700 BC (H-S, 242).
Plate 16:2	Small Proto-Corinthian oil jug, around 630 BC (H-S, 250).
Plate 17:1	Seal from Uruk period, Mesopotamia. (Cr, 149).
Plate 17:2	Stela segment from Ur, Mesopotamia, Neo-Sumerian period (Cr, 150).
Plate 17:3	Fresco segment from Mari, beginning of 17th century BC (Cr, 151).
Plate 17:4	Mycenaean ring seal, 1400-1300 BC (Cr, 164).
Plate 17:5	Mycenaean ring seal, 1400-1300 BC (Cr, 165).
Plate 17:6	Mycenaean sphinx fashioned in ceramic, around 1300 BC (Cr, 106).
Plate 17: 7	Fresco segments from Pylos, around 1200 BC (Cr, 108).
Plate 18	"Wild Goat Style" Oinochoe from Rhodes, beginning of 6th century BC. (Br, 43 = Boardman 1975, fig. 44).
Plate 19:1-2	A line of ivory lotus petals (used as accessory handles) from Nimrud, 9th century BC (Barnett 1957 Pl. LXXXI, S. 275-77).
Plate 19:3	Ivory Phoenician panel, Nimrud, 9th century BC (Barnett 1957, Pl. III, C.4).
Plate 19:4	Female gryphon feeding its young. Hammered bronze plate from Olympia, end of 7th century BC (Br, 48; H-S, 170).
Plate 20:1	Proto-Attic ceramic plate from Kerameikos, Athens, 670 BC. Ceramic copy of a Phoenician metal model (Mar, Comp. 16 = Markoe 1985, fig-Comp.16).
Plate 20:2	Bronze plate from Kerameikos, Athens, 850-750 BC (Mar, G1).
Plate 20:3	Bronze plate from Fortetsa, Crete, 750-700BC (Mar, Cr1).
Plate 21:1-2	Bronze plate from Delphi, 750-700 BC (Mar, G4).
Plate 22:1	Bronze plate, most probably from Sparta, 750-700 BC (Mar, G8)
Plate 22:2	Bronze plate from Nimrud, 8th century BC (Mar, Comp. 3).
Plate 23:1	Plate detail from plate 41:1-2 (Mar, G4 (detail)).
Plate 23:2	Bronze plate, most probably from Olympia, 750-700 BC (Mar, G7).
Plate 24:1-2	Bronze plate from Olympia, 750-700 BC (Mar, G3).
Plate 25:1	Fragment from bronze plate from Olympia, 750-700 BC (Mar, G3).
Plate 25:2	Silver plate from Idalion, Cyprus. 710-675 BC (Mar, Cy1).
Plate 26:1	Silver plate from Idalion, Cyprus, 710-675 BC (Mar, Cy2).
Plate 26:2	Silver plate from Kourion, Cyprus, gold plated figures, 710-675 BC (Mar, Cy8).
Plate 27:1-2	Bronze plate from Kerameikos, Athens, 850-750 BC (Mar, G1).
Plate 27:3	Gold plate from Ugarit, 15th-14th centuries BC (Moscati 1988:440).
Plate 28:1	Frieze from a Krater (Heraion compound, temple of Hera) in Samos, made of terracotta. Beginning of 7th century BC (H-S, 113).

Plate 28:2   Attic ceramic drinking cup, 720-700 BC (H-S, 241).

Plate 28:3   Painting on conical base of Dinos vessel, around 700 BC (H-S, 244).

Plate 29:1-2 Dinos vessel from Arcades, Crete, mid 7th century BC (H-S, 253-254).

Plate 30:1-4 Bronze Gryphon heads (attached to the vessels at the base of their necks) from Samos (1-2) and Olympia (3-4), first half of 7th century BC (H-S 405-8).

Plate 30:5   Ceramic Cycladic jug, mid 7th century BC (Br, 44 = Boardman 1975, fig. 44).

Plate 30:6   Fragment of Cycladic Pythos jar, second quarter of 7th century BC (H-S, 412).

Plate 31:1-2 Statuette of kneeling lion holding a perfume bowl, made of clay from Arcades Crete, third quarter of 7th century BC (H-S, 447-448).

Plate 32:1   Proto-Corinthian Aryballos (a view from the top), half of 7th century BC (Dunbabin 1962:39, 228).

Plate 32:2   Proto-Corinthian Aryballos, around 720 BC (Br, 34).

Plate 33:1   Bronze kriophorus statuette from Crete. Last quarter of 7th century BC. (Boardman 1996, fig. 46).

Plate 33:2   Statue of goddess known as: "The Auxerre Goddess", probably from Crete. Around 630 BC (Boardman 1996, fig. 28; H-S, 438).

Plate 33:3   Bronze statuette of a woman from Thebes. Third quarter of 7th century BC (Boardman 1996, 48).

Plate 34:1-3 Phoenician style ivory panels from Nimrud, 9th century BC (Barnett 1957, Pl. IV, C.12, C.14-15).

Plate 34:4   Stone relief of woman's head from the acropolis in Mycenae in Cretan-Oriental style. Around 630 BC (Boardman 1996, fig. 35).

Plate 34:5   Stone relief of woman's head from Malesina, Boeotia, end of 7th century BC (Boardman 1996, fig. 36).

PLATE 1

1

2

3

4

5

6

7

8

9

10

11

12

13

PLATE 2

1

2

3

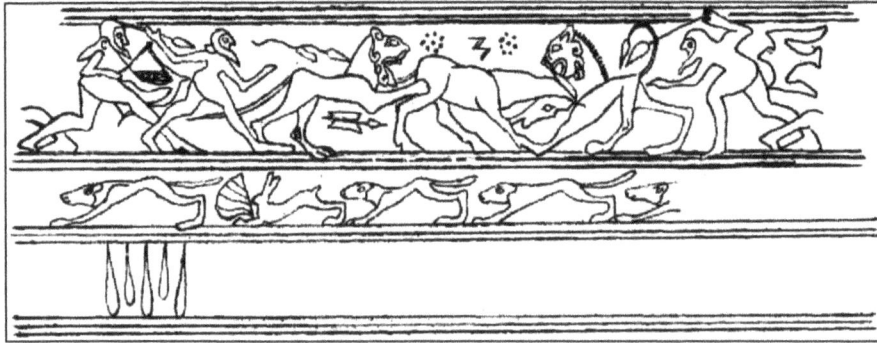

4

5

6

7a

7b

7c

PLATE 3

1

2

3

4

5

6

PLATE 4

1

2

3

4

5

6

7

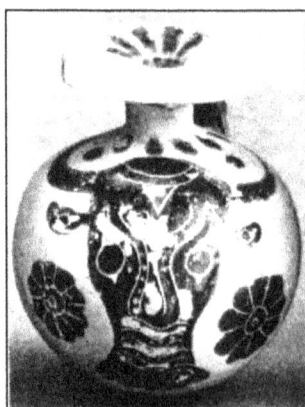

8

9

10a

10b

10c

10d

PLATE 5

1

2

3

4

5a

5b

6

7

65

PLATE 6

1

2

3

4

5

PLATE 7

1

2

3

4

5

6

7

8

PLATE 8

1

2

5

3

4

PLATE 9

1

2

PLATE 10

1

2

3

PLATE 11

1

2

3

4

PLATE 12

1

2

3

4

PLATE 13

1

2

3

4

PLATE 14

1   2   3

4

PLATE 15

1

2

3

4

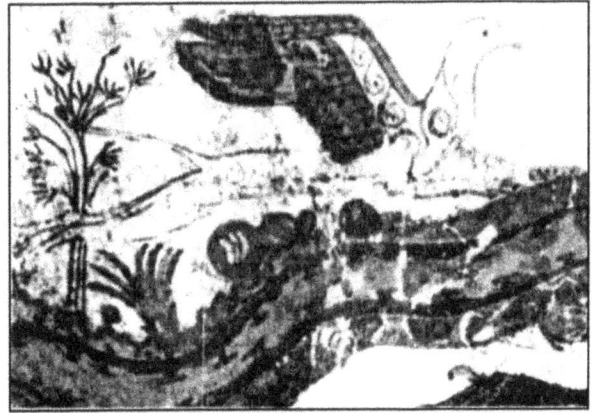

5

6

7

PLATE 16

1a

1b

2

PLATE 17

1

3

2

4

5

SPHINX

III B

1

6

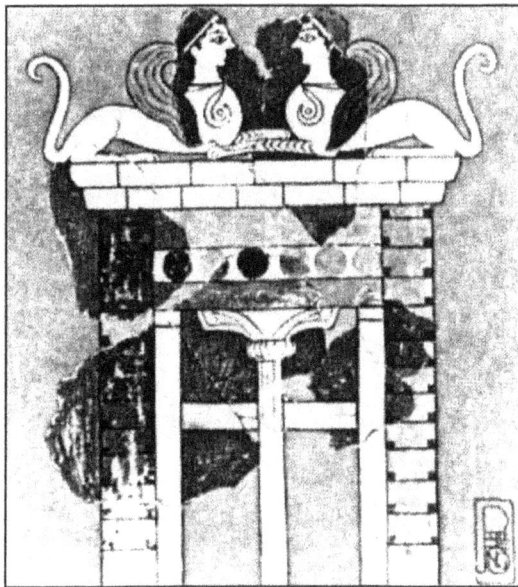

7

PLATE 18

1

PLATE 19

1

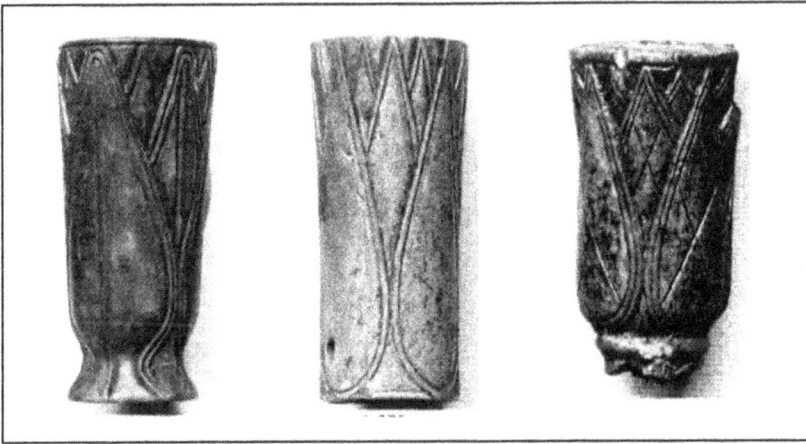

2

3

4

PLATE 20

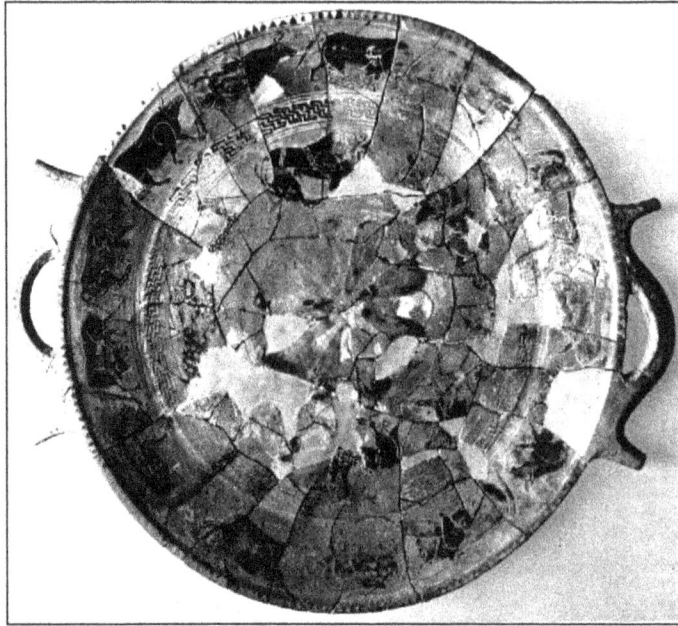

1

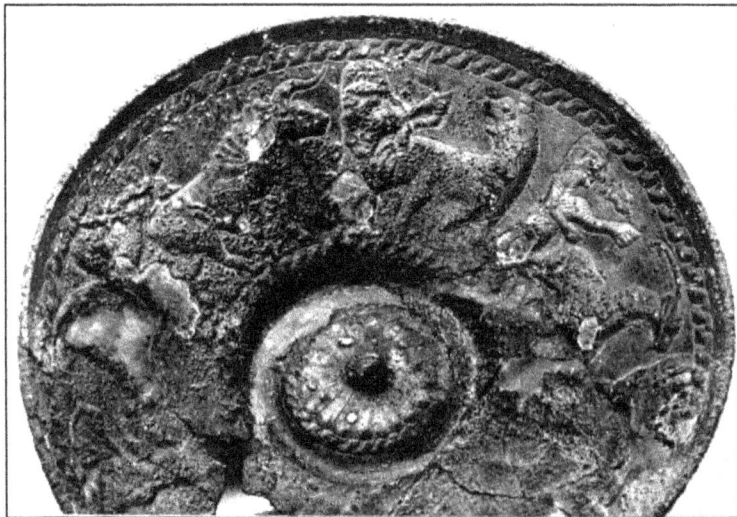

2

3

PLATE 21

1

2

PLATE 22

1

2

PLATE 23

1

2

PLATE 24

1

2

PLATE 25

1

2

PLATE 26

1

2

PLATE 27

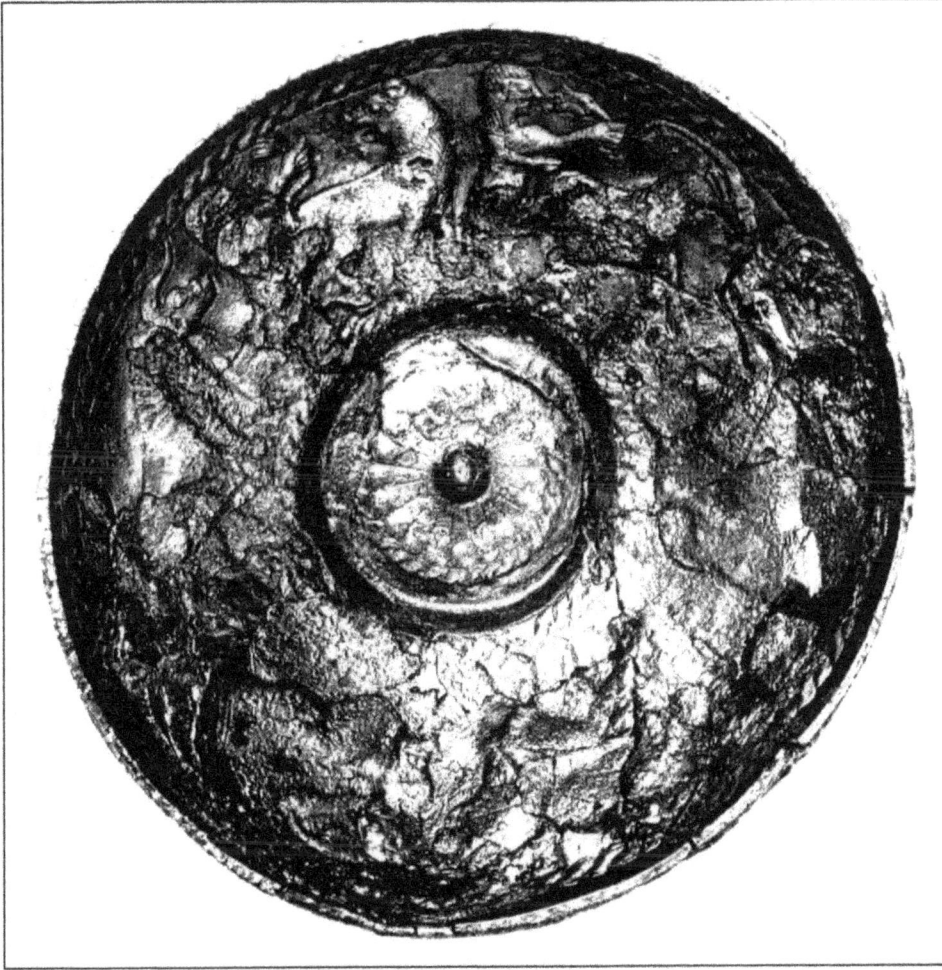

1

2

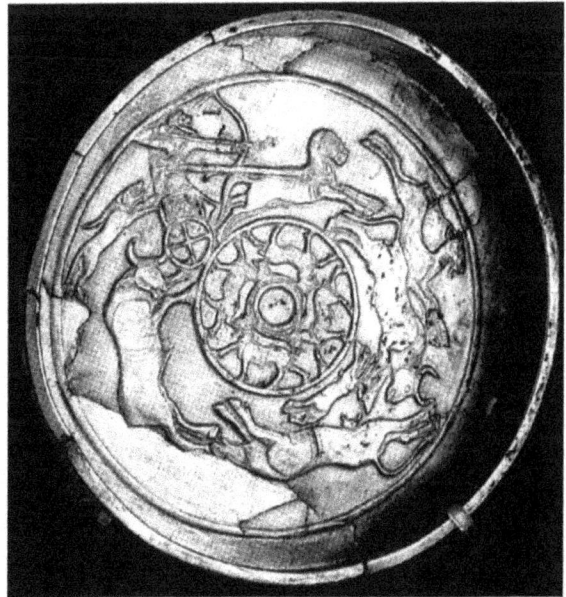

3

PLATE 28

1

2

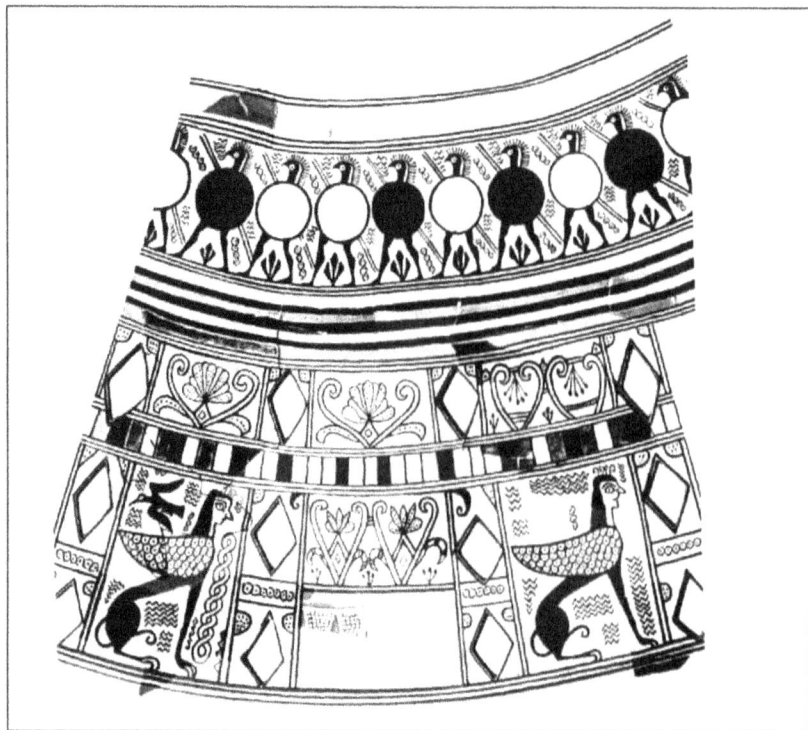

3

PLATE 29

1

2

PLATE 30

1

2

3

4

5

6

PLATE 31

1

2

PLATE 32

1

2

PLATE 33

1   2   3

PLATE 34

1

2

3

4

5

www.ingramcontent.com/pod-product-compliance
Lightning Source LLC
Chambersburg PA
CBHW061301270326
41932CB00029B/3428